To: Ayssi
Thanks for your support
and your interest in social
justice!

INSIDE FERGUSON

A VOICE FOR THE VOICELESS

DEVIN S. JAMES

INSIDE FERGUSON

A VOICE FOR THE VOICELESS

DESTINY
PUBLISHING

Destiny Publishing
1819 SW 5th Ave #350
Portland, Oregon 97201

booking@DevinSJames.com

www.DestinyPublishingCo.com
www.insideferguson.com

Cover Photo by: www.RomanRivera.com
Cover Design by: www.KoerCreative.com and www.DevinSJames.com

FIRST EDITION

Library of Congress Cataloging-in-Publication Data is available upon request.

ISBN 978-0-9966488-0-6

971-470-7943

To the people who have been victimized
by law enforcement,
the people who swore to protect them.

CONTENTS

CONTENTS

CONTENTS

ACKNOWLEDGEMENTS

FIRST AND FOREMOST, I have to give all thanks to God. I know I have a purpose and that my life matters because of the most high. None of this would have been possible had he not guided me and protected me through it all.

To my mom, thank you for sacrificing so much of your life for me and my siblings. I can never repay you; I love you mom.

To my dad, you are the strongest person I know. Now I have the lens to see who you really are. You're a champion. I love you pop.

To my children, Devin Jr. and Jasmine-Christi, thank you for giving me your unconditional love. Thanks for being the most awesome travel buddies and for keeping a smile on my face during the difficult times. You both inspire me to be the best person and dad I can be. I love you.

To Alicia Renee', you helped record the details that paved the way for me to develop the outline for this book. I couldn't have done any of this without you. I want you to know that your efforts, your generosity, your love, and friendship mean everything to me.

To Rita Days, I could never thank you enough for the unwavering support and the love you've shown me since I came to Missouri. Your guidance was instrumental in my success and I thank you for being who you are to me and the black community in STL.

To Barbara Cooper, you helped me in my darkest hour when I was going through the legal process and during my time in prison. When I got out you continued to support me and lobbied not just for Memphis, but for the world to give me a second chance. Thank you for being you and for continuing to support me.

To Bob Herman, my attorney: when no attorney in Missouri would take the case to defend my company for fear of becoming victim of the political witch hunt you stepped up and agreed to represent me. You help me to understand what happened to my company and the people in Ferguson from a legal perspective and I want to thank you for helping me fight for justice

To my team at the Devin James Group and all the subcontractors, we have been through a lot and you have all received unjust persecutions just because of me, I want to tell you I'm sorry for the impact my past had on your lives and I want to thank all of you for the strength you displayed when we were challenged on our mission – communication that benefits people. I'm particularly grateful to Matthew T. Nebel, thank you for your efforts and for being such a team player.

To my true friends, those of you who disregarded the constant negative attacks against my character, thank you for standing by my side every day.

Author's Note

THIS BOOK IS BASED on my experiences, those of my team at the Devin James Group and those of members of St. Louis County, with whom I worked tirelessly in the volatile period after Ferguson police officer Darren Wilson shot and killed Michael Brown, Jr. on August 9, 2014. The conversations revealed are based on memories, experiences, e-mails, text messages, audio recordings and transcriptions of events as they unfolded. I recall the events here with as much accuracy as my memory and tangible documents permit. The conversations in this book are meant to expose the extreme difficulty in navigating through the murky fog of race, division, false leadership, and intense fear that one faces in order to work in the best interest of the African American community.

Specifically, this book aims to point out the inability of white leaders in Ferguson to effectively advocate for their black residents. This inability stems from a culture of white supremacy and superiority, in which black lives hold no substance or value. A deeply embedded system of white supremacy in America allows whites to benefit from institutional racism and bias, while simultaneously denying their racist tendencies. This proverbial veil from race-based problems and issues provides or, until recently provided, a screen behind which black humanity is pushed into the background, creating a harsh racial environment for black communities. Michael Brown's death ripped this veil apart in front of the whole world, exposing grave institutional disparities and a long history of racism in the United States.

Many white Americans, including those in Ferguson, fail to realize the historical and institutional components of racism that grant them the ability to blatantly ignore the large racial disparities and injustices around them. This is white privilege at work. White privilege creates a strange form of equilibrium for white Americans, in which one can rally against racism as an individual function, while concurrently ignoring the organizational dynamics that shape and mold racism as an oppressive system, built to destroy non-white lives and identities.

In America, white ideals and standards are deemed as 'beautiful', 'good', and 'acceptable'. In Ferguson, I challenged these notions by asking questions that challenged white racial identity. Although many leaders vocalized their opposition to racism, their actions revealed both an incompetence to truly connect with black issues and a fear of being pushed out of their safe, dominant world. Many people cowered when forced to stare racism in the eyes, and realized their part in benefiting from white supremacy.

I spent my time in Ferguson as a voice for the voiceless, ensuring that members of the local government heard from the black community. The government exhibited many of the problems consistent with white privilege – claiming an organizational opposition to racism, while exhibiting an incapability to deal with racism's real roots. Making this apparent was our arduous journey; this book shows the many challenges—and triumphs—that our group encountered along the way.

INTRODUCTION

ON AUGUST 9, 2014, 18-year-old Michael Brown, Jr. was shot and killed by a police officer in Ferguson, Missouri. Within hours, this horrible event quickly became the center story throughout both national and international media. Brown, an unarmed black male, was shot six times by Darren Wilson, a white police officer. The racial dynamic surrounding Brown's murder sparked an emotional wildfire among black and white communities, both in Ferguson and across the country.

Every fire has a spark, and for Ferguson's black community, that spark was Mike Brown's death. If we all take a step back and remove all of the media coverage, press releases, and social media, it's really not difficult to see why the spark ignited a raging conflagration.

Most people fail to remember that Michael Brown's death was a tragedy. Brown was someone's son, someone's cousin, someone's friend and someone's student. Forget what side you're on. At the end of the day, this is the death of a young man. This is a future that was taken away. Right or wrong, it is a death that deserves to be mourned.

It is important to note that the black community represents 70% of Ferguson's population. Accordingly, all Ferguson businesses and corporations, from gas stations to retail chains and restaurants, gain the majority of their revenue from the black dollar. Although these corporations line their pockets from black consumer habits, not one entity made a gesture in support of their largest client base during the Michael Brown tragedy.

From my own experiences both in and around Ferguson, it seemed that Michael's humanity was often disregarded in the media blitz surrounding his death. It was evident that many of the officials I worked with, and those in charge at the time, lacked the cultural sensitivity needed to properly engage Ferguson's black community in response to such a tragedy. Executives from the public relations (PR) firms working for Ferguson failed to see Michael's death for the tragedy that it was. Corporate executives had lost all empathy and weren't concerned about the black community, who invested daily in their respective businesses. The executives treated the black community as if it no longer served value, but was, rather, like a dog that had bitten its owner.

I am the founder of the Devin James Group, a nationally recognized minority-owned communications firm. The Devin James Group served as one entity in a group of public relations firms tasked to assist Ferguson, Missouri from January 2014 to November 2014.

Our experience was a tedious one. I remember Molotov cocktails crashing into the street, then tear gas poisoning the eye sockets and nostrils of protesters and camera crews alike. I remember masses of people, black and white, scattering in confusion as they ran for their lives. I remember how, in that moment of panic, they all blurred together and looked the same.

But beneath the surface, where tensions were extreme, the world was still divided.

In order to understand what is truly happening in Ferguson, it is important to look at the history of St. Louis, Missouri. A most poignant example of historical context comes from the *Dred Scott v. Sanford* decision, in which the Supreme Court ruled that black people were not considered citizens, but, rather, as property, under the Constitution.[1] Dred Scott, a St. Louis native, attempted to gain his freedom several times in the Missouri courts and failed.[2] This decision both solidified and excused white brutality toward black lives, by (further) writing into law that blacks were considered as property – as inhuman.

Although modern practices have wiped the *Dred Scott* decision away from the law books, we are left with the mental residue of the Supreme Court's dark, racist decision. We see this cultural poison seep into the lives and actions of many modern-day law enforcement officials. A quick timeline reveals the chilling reality of black men and women in America: Milwaukee's Dontre Hamilton (shot 14 times by a police officer in a park), New York's Eric Garner (killed by an illegal chokehold by NYPD officers), Chicago's Rekia Boyd (shot by a Chicago Police Department officer who mistook her boyfriend's cellphone for a gun), the recent death of Sandra Bland (who was arrested by a Texas State Trooper and mysteriously died while in custody), and many more. This epidemic of black death by police, put on display by the influx of modern technology and cellphone cameras, is not new to any part of the country. From the hellish, devilish jaws of slavery, to violence against blacks during non-violent marches in the 1960's, to today's police killings, tensions be-

---

[1] *Dred Scott v. Sandford*, 60 U.S. 393.
[2] *Historic Missourians*. The State Historical Society of Missouri. http://shs.umsystem.edu/historicmissourians/name/s/scottd/

tween blacks and law enforcement have always been high (despite what media outlets portray as a 'new emergence'.) Missouri is not alone in its cry for justice – the whole country sings the same song, swelling with emotion and searching for peace.

Since the Michael Brown tragedy, the riots have subsided, but the tension between the city and its people has remained. Trust, an element corroded since slavery times, does not exist between white Ferguson law enforcement officials and the black population that Ferguson police are slated to serve. Nearly all of the officials governing Ferguson are white; while Ferguson is a predominantly black community. When coupled with the deep-seated history of racism in St. Louis and St. Louis County (think about the implications of *Dred Scott* on the area,) it is nearly impossible for the black community to feel like anyone in power can relate to them. This serves as a large reason for the unrest.

I came to Ferguson to develop a community engagement plan that would help fill this void (or, at least, that was my original task.) At the time of the Michael Brown tragedy, my firm was called in to assist the two white public relations firms working for the City of Ferguson. Our job was to develop a community engagement strategy to help the public relations firms working with Ferguson reestablish relationships with the African American community, and to communicate more effectively with members of the community who were protesting, both peacefully and violently. For weeks, my firm stood as the only communications link between the two sides.

My team worked tirelessly to provide effective, beneficial communication strategies to Ferguson officials. We believe that equity, transparency, and humility are the key ingredients to effective communication, regardless of what spectators and commentators say. Effective communication is essential to creating a strategy that truly benefits all people. We're not just a communications firm that sweeps up after everyone and stages the dirty house to look clean. We're agents of change, who get dirty doing the work that we love every day.

After months of hard work, my firm was suddenly released from our contract, released for the media to gnash at my reputation, and then left in the dust, my reputation in tatters. After establishing my firm in the market for over six years, having represented small and large-scale clients from each end of the state, I suddenly lost my brand. My name no longer carried any substance or weight. I had to dig my feet into the soil, claw back, regroup, and gain the intestinal fortitude needed to move forward. Despite this, the community engagement plan that I developed (which included a leadership transition plan for Ferguson) was still being used by the other firms. Now those firms, corrupt elected officials, Ferguson officials and the Department of Justice were receiving all of the credit. I had been played as a pawn in their own selfish scheme.

Those times still pass through my mind often. They affected every aspect of my life, and they are nearly impossible to ignore. PTSD (Post-Traumatic Stress Disorder) lingers over my shoulder often—even driving through the same streets brings back those same stinging sensations I felt then. After making it through that tragic period in my life after Ferguson, and re-establishing my business and brand, I decided to tell my side of the story.

My purpose is to inform those who have been misinformed, to educate those who have been immersed in the ignorance, the deception, the corporate greed and political agendas, and to inspire those like me, who know that we can overcome any obstacle that is placed in our way. It is my hope that through this book, we can stop trivializing the death of Michael Brown and see his death as the tragedy it was. I aim to identify the mistakes made in handling the tragedy, and start the dialogue needed to create changes nationwide--in all municipalities and at every level of government throughout our country.

Most of all, I am writing this book to inspire a willingness in ourselves to recognize our own shortcomings, admit our wrongdoings, forgive people for their wrongdoings and cooperate to bring about positive change in all communities.

At the very least, I hope that this piece starts the conversation.

INSIDE FERGUSON

CHAPTER 1

I AM MIKE BROWN

KEEPING A SPARE TIRE

A CRISIS CAN HAPPEN anywhere, at any time, to anyone. Think of a time that you were in a crisis. Maybe you overslept, and you were afraid of getting fired from work. Maybe you were afraid of missing an important deadline for a huge contract that you know you could win. Maybe you or a loved one was diagnosed with an illness. You may not know it, but you are highly experienced in crisis forecasting. Some may say that you're an expert.

Crisis forecasting is surprisingly common. Perhaps you've watched Shark Tank's Mark Cuban repeatedly reject entrepreneurs due to a poor articulation of their startup business's revenue potential. As a contestant on the show, you conduct additional research on Mark Cuban's portfolio preferences on the night before your marketing pitch. You watch tons of reruns to familiarize yourself with the process, and by using the "buzz words" he's accustomed to, you develop a counterargument to anything he could say to reject funding your startup.

On a night before going to work or going to school, you set an alarm so you won't oversleep. When you get in your car, you put on your seatbelt in case of an accident, and you keep a spare tire in the trunk in case of a flat.

Crisis forecasting is all about being prepared in advance -- having those "spare tires" with you so you can avoid sitting helplessly on the side of the road. In my field of work, keeping a "spare tire" involves assessing a situation and researching all possible crises that could arise from any given department within an organization. I am trained to develop both a worst case and "what if" scenario model. When every possible crisis is identified, you start to plan your own spare tires so that you can keep moving forward when the crisis does come -- and trust me, it inevitably will.

Crisis forecasting is always a part of our lives. Sometimes it's small, like setting an alarm for the morning, but it sometimes can present itself on a much larger stage.

Universally, however, we know that when a big crisis comes, it takes heart, courage, honesty, and integrity to step into the fire to manage it. Like a fireman, we need prior experience in addition to bravery in order to successfully fight raging fires; we need to have a certain level of physical and emotional conditioning in order to deal with large crises in our lives. You have to be built to withstand the fire and be tested in every way to perform crisis management services. This line of work is not for the faint of heart.

Unfortunately, it didn't seem anyone I worked with, inside or outside of Ferguson, possessed any of those qualities during my time as their communications consultant.

TRIVIALIZED TRAGEDIES
AND RUINED REPUTATIONS

On the day of Michael Brown's death, his body lay in the street for about four hours. Strangely, neither the PR firms, nor most of the city officials could see how demoralizing it was for Brown's body to lie in the street so long after he was gunned down. Instead, the firms tried to put out the fire with high-level campaigns aimed only at defending their actions, maintaining the objectives of their corporate stakeholders, creating more revenue for their firms, preserving their reputations, and making false attempts to appease the black community and to appear concerned. The uprising resulting from Michael's death was seen as a threat to Ferguson's reputation, and many people saw the black community as a threat to their livelihood. Instead of taking the blame for any blunders, standing up, and admitting their wrongdoings, my former client(s) and their public relations firms chose to create scapegoats for the media to attack. (I eventually became one of those scapegoats).

When the story of my past came to national attention, I was fired from my position. Everything changed. My firm and I were fired as subcontractors to the other firms. My past was publicized, reworded, modified, torn to shreds, and taped together to create a narrative that didn't exist. Suddenly, I was seen as a token Negro working for the oppressors of the black community in Ferguson. I knew that this wasn't true–I knew that I had always been working for the people and was placed in the media as a distraction from the real issues. I literally had to crawl my way back to redemption–not only for myself, but also for my firm and the people who depended on me. My former client(s) and their PR firms that I had partnered with had decided to operate under their own selfish motives, and used me as a pawn in their twisted game. I endured severe personal attacks on my character, professionalism and intellectual competency. As a result, I was blackballed and lost every contract my firm held in the state of Missouri.

The people I worked for thought they were saving themselves from further public humiliation. What they didn't realize was that I had been the only one doing anything positive for the community all along. The City of Ferguson realized that, and immediately requested that I return to work directly with them. This was because Ferguson leadership saw first-hand how my insight improved their thought processes and interactions, in spite of the media's pointed attack on my character. My insight eventually improved Ferguson officials' relationships with the black community, despite the corruption occurring at every turn during the tragedy.

The reason I want to expose the wrongdoing in Ferguson is because this behavior happens regularly in government agencies and corporations alike, across the country. As a contractor with over eleven years of experience in working for several municipalities and state entities, I've noticed a trend about Ferguson. In the wake of August 2014, many people loved to point fingers at Ferguson, attempting to point out how "different" they are. In comparison by doing this, these entities are not realizing that the same corruption, implicit bias, and institutional racism exists within their own institutions. Ferguson received lots of attention, but Ferguson is not unique. Michael Brown's story received a lot of attention, but sadly, Michael Brown's tale is not unique. As mentioned in the Introduction, similar things are happening to my black brothers and sisters across the country at a rapid-fire pace.

THE REAL DEVIN JAMES

There are days of my youth that I would rather forget, if it were at all possible. I possess both physical and emotional scars as a result of things I did, things that happened around me, and things that have happened to me. I have only shared these experiences with family, a few close friends and my therapist, and if it weren't for their relevance to this story, I would keep them to myself. It is my hope that unveiling my background will explain my own ties with the Ferguson community, with black Americans generally, and with Michael Brown himself. I hope that my story will reinforce the cries of frustration and anger in underserved minority communities, which are only beginning to be heard. I also hope that it reflects the strength, focus and dedication needed to rise from a poverty-ridden environment to experience success as a business owner, brand strategist, and communications consultant.

I was raised in a single parent home in Memphis, Tennessee. From the time I was about two years old to age 12, my father served time in prison, while my mother raised my four siblings and me. I was raised in a city nestled in the Deep South, the home of where they praise one king (Elvis) and killed another (Martin Luther King, Jr.). When you visit Memphis, you feel the presence and legacy of Elvis, but Memphis does not give that same respect and feeling for Brother King. Memphis has always been a racially divided city. Racism resided in Memphis before I did, crept its way into my life and affairs after my birth, and continues to rear its ugly head today.

My dad was a revolving door in my life. He was present sporadically, but he mostly stayed out of my life. He was doing what he had to do to survive with the resources given to him. Like many black men, he too lost his father at a young age – not to the system designed to trap black men, but to death. Shortly after losing his father, his mother died, and he turned to the streets to make a name for himself.

Simply put, my father was a hustler. Many disregard the value of street savvy, but his way of life proved to have an enormous impact on my life and future. I met my father's street persona for the first time when I was around 12 years old. I saw the way he presented himself, how he commanded respect of everyone he met. He was charismatic, and a natural ladies' man. It wasn't long before I began emulating him. I learned how a black man should be every day -- "dressed for success." My dad always had the best-looking wardrobe: it wasn't about expensive brands, but he had a natural eye for style and knew how suits should be tailored to fit you. No matter where he was, he made sure that people took notice. That was a part of his personal brand. My father served as my first course in personal branding.

While sitting in on a lecture by author and Harvard professor David B. Yoffie, I realized that my father was a marketing and business development genius. Unbeknownst to him, I was his protégé, and he was teaching me everything I needed to later develop the Devin James Group. My father learned the skills of a CEO by being thrust into insurmountable circumstances and having to make critical decisions at a young age. Lacking formal education, but still wanting to teach and groom me into a businessman, he provided an experienced-based learning approach for me in which he was the case study.

Although my father was a natural businessman and marketer, he struggled in his relationship with my mother. As a result, my parents had a rough relationship. It is important to remember the time period as added context into my family's issues, as the 1980's served as the cultural face of the impact of drugs, mass incarceration, and drug sentencing disparities on the African-American community and its families. My parents were no exception. When my dad was gone, my mom would try to shelter me from him. During those off times, she never really talked about him, and she would change the subject when I brought him up. As a child, it felt like she didn't want him to exist. She would become noticeably angry whenever my curiosity about him would surface. Our exchanges resulted in a weird set of dynamics that I never understood. My parents loved each other deeply; they had an intense passion, but the fights were just as intense. Whenever my dad would show up, our family would be better off. While I truly appreciate everything my mother did for us, because she sacrificed her life and career for our well-being, we didn't struggle because of the "deadbeat dad" trope. My father did what he could to support us even while he was in jail.

My experience with my father, coupled with later experiences in life, taught me that when a black man goes to jail, he is automatically labeled a "deadbeat." The black man's family likely disowns him after the reality of a long sentence sets in. My father fell into this stereotype, although he still supported us and sent money from behind prison walls.

My mother didn't want us to think that my dad contributed while in prison. I suppose she thought it would make her seem like less of an authority figure – like money directly correlated to value. My siblings and I didn't care about that. Eventually, she started down a dark path of denial and abuse, which caused my oldest brother and sister (to whom I was closest) to run away.

Instantly, I felt alone. I had no father, no mother, my two best friends and role models were gone, and I had no answers. When my dad finally left for the last time I found out, then, what it meant to be at the bottom.

Our circumstances nosedived for the worse, and we never had any guests in our home that were actually human. Our only company was rats and roaches. Some nights I heard them, I felt them, and I couldn't sleep. My empty stomach rumbled and rattled, reaching past my intestines to touch my back. I could not hide from the fact that I lived in abject poverty. My mother did all that she could, but she couldn't afford to feed us. Food stamps weren't enough to feed five kids. I began stealing from stores to get food, water, clothing, and whatever else we needed. We couldn't cook because we had no money to pay the utilities, so we constantly ate fast food and junk from corner stores. In fact, I never attended the 4th and 5th grade in elementary because we were so poor.

I still remember the day that I snuck into a hardware store on South Third Street off of Mallory. I stole a garden hose and brought it home. That night, I hooked it up to our neighbor's spigot and filled a bucket with water so we could wash up. I boiled whatever water we had left using a stolen kerosene heater, and that served as our water supply for the next day.

Throughout my childhood, I was labeled a 'problem child' by MCS (Memphis City Schools) due to my conduct issues; however, I still managed to make good grades in school. Truthfully, I was bored, and the curriculum was painstakingly redundant. I was largely uninterested, the black history that teachers taught in school was completely inaccurate, and the core of their learning model wasn't relevant to my trajectory. I eventually decided to opt out, as many modern-day parents choose for their children today. Maybe I was bad, maybe the system failed me, and maybe I was setup to fail; who knows? I do definitively know that I was labeled, and that very labeling barred me from several opportunities.

When I finally got a chance to go to a better school (Ridgeway High), I viewed it as a second chance. I loved Ridgeway. The experience was both great and scary at the same time. It was the first time I had been in a predominantly middle to upper-middle class, black and white student, but majority white environment. I loved that I could join the marching band, chess team, debate team, or whatever team I wished to join. It was such a different learning experience than the schools I had been to. Most of my classmates and staff at the school didn't know I was homeless the entire time I attended Ridgeway.

At the time, I felt that middle-class people were rich. I wasn't rich by any means, and I took offense when the rich kids would pick on me because of my socioeconomic status. Most times, if a scuffle occurred between another student and myself, I was the only one who was punished. If it weren't for Brian Pollard, son of Andrew and Rose Pollard (the owners of A&R BBQ, a landmark restaurant in the city), I wouldn't have made it. I would leave school every day, catch the MATA bus back to South Memphis, and Brian would let me work as many hours as I could, so that I would have a safe place to do my homework, rest, and eat. Even though I had a strained relationship with my mom, I would never let that get in the way of doing what I could to help out. I didn't want my little brother to experience the same hardships I did, and I worked to ensure that he saw better days. Brian saw how hard I worked and gave me food for my family, so that I wouldn't have to spend money to feed everyone. Brian's love for me was unwarranted, and to this day, I don't know why he showed me so much love. Brian's family also loved and supported me, and, for a while, I felt that I had a home away from home.

Despite Brian and his family's love and support, however, the ills of my own world quickly became too much to bear. I was sent to an alternative school after being jumped in a gang fight. There, I was again jumped by a group of gang members – this time, for being unaffiliated.

During alternative school, another fight occurred that would change my course in life. I was stabbed repeatedly during a gang fight, along with several other wounded people. In a quick-witted move of self-defense, I grabbed a knife from one of the gang members and used it to defend myself against the growing mob. After that fight, I was expelled from MCS entirely. I escaped assault charges from the Memphis Police Department based on eyewitness testimonies supporting my argument that someone else was the aggressor.

At this point, I was tired of fighting. I fought for my food; I fought for water, for my education, and for my life while in school. I often compared our life to my father's. Even though he was in and out of prison, he seemed to live the good life. Most importantly, he never seemed to let life's circumstances get the best of him. He maintained a keen mental strength. The allure of his lifestyle was enough to attract me to the streets. I didn't understand the risk, but I felt like I had nothing to lose. Before long, I decided to become a hustler myself. To me, the only difference between a street hustler and an "entrepreneur" was legitimacy.

After that last fight, I joined a gang for protection.

Protecting myself wasn't just about keeping me from getting my ass beat every day; it was about joining a brotherhood, in addition to enjoying added protection from other ills. At that time in my life, it felt like bad things just kept happening. Think Murphy's Law – anything that can go wrong, will go wrong. There were several experiences that led me to this decision. I was robbed and stabbed when just getting off a bus to go to work; I'd been slashed by a knife multiple times across my chest during a gang fight. For many reasons, some sort of affiliation had to happen. I didn't feel safe. I didn't have a home. My real brothers didn't protect me much, and were too caught up in their own lives to give me the attention I needed. I couldn't even blame them for trying to escape our lives anyway they could. My sister and oldest brother, along with myself, walked away from

DEVIN JAMES

our family because of my mother's abuse. As a result, I no longer had my own siblings or my mom looking after me. As a high school dropout and staring homelessness directly into the face, I had some major decisions to make.

Joining a gang wasn't on my to-do list prior to being in the streets, but I had a deep need to belong to something. I wanted to belong to a group—much like college individuals wish to join fraternal and other professional organizations in order to belong. These organizations provide many students with a social "home" of sorts. They help to shape the social experiences that most college students have, because the students have the opportunity to surround themselves with people of similar values. Just like a college student, I wanted to experience family, a heightened level of protection, and a brotherhood.

My gang consisted of various hustlers and older drug dealers. I chose this group because it was the only option that would allow me to stay virtually unknown, but would also allow me to be amongst other groups without risk. In the hierarchy of the streets, drugs and money were always above gangs (or "sets") in Memphis. Colors, rituals, the neighborhood Crips, G's, Bloods or Vice Lords all respected the hustlers and drug dealers. Some of them were gang members themselves; others were just on a mission that everyone respected. Because of my elders, I was blessed with the immunity that allowed me to build relationships around the country.

Life for me was never easy, but I never considered myself a victim. I used the only option I had available at the time. The words of my father often rang in my ear: "When you are in a situation where you have no other options, you need to change your perspective and your location." After being homeless for months, I weighed the options of a shelter or enrolling in Job Corps as my only ways off the streets. The Memphis Job Corp Center, posthumously renamed the Benjamin L. Hooks Job Corp Center, served as an escape for all of the craziness going on in my life.

After beginning Job Corps, it only took me two weeks to complete the Electronic Assembly Program and to pass the High School Equivalency Test, both of which were required to get my GED. Because I didn't meet the state of Tennessee's minimum age requirement, my admission counselor made it possible for me to go the Batesville Job Corps Center in Mississippi. I was able to obtain my GED through this program.

At that point, my life was a real rollercoaster. At the same time I obtained my GED, I was months away from the birth of my first daughter. I diligently tried to pull things together to be in a better position to raise her. As the pregnancy went on, I grew fonder of this new role I found myself in. I spoke to my girlfriend's belly and had sweet conversations with my daughter. My girlfriend and I dreamed of how one day, we could do what was best for our baby girl. We both grew up in single parent households, so even though we were young, uneducated and naïve, we believed that we could turn things around for our daughter.

We named her Destiny.

On May 22, 2000 at 12:40 AM, I showed up at the Regional Medical Center ready to be the father I never had. My heart stopped when I heard the news. My baby was already dead. My princess, my joy, my six pounds and seven ounces of beauty was taken away from me. Destiny LaSha never even took a breath – she was stillborn. I never saw her. We were unmarried teenagers, so I was coldly handed a piece of paper with her footprints and a death certificate and asked to leave. I wasn't even allowed to sign paperwork to give her my last name.

Before long, I was a fully committed to being a hustler. I wasn't going to strive for a career that would take 40 years of my life working just to pay for school and a decent neighborhood to live in. At the time, I thought that my daughter had died because we were too poor to have quality healthcare. That thought gave me all the incentive to do things my way and succeed. The experience was demoralizing, but solidified the fact that success was the only option for both my future family and myself.

My friends all had a different track to success than I. My friends are sons and daughters of political figures, small business owners, moguls, entertainers, and the like. I inherited nothing but heartache and hardships. Just like any other individual, I was looking to make a name for myself, and worked within my skill set to make it happen. Because I am a black man, I am evaluated much more harshly for my decisions than a white person in the same position. Although Steve Jobs likely didn't have as rough of an upbringing as I, he still dropped out of school and became one of the biggest technology moguls in the world. My decision to leave school and to use what I knew to survive is a similar story to Jobs', but my experience has been laden with poverty-related challenges. Changing my life, however, is not a story championed like the story of Steve Jobs because of the very barriers put in place by society to set me, and people who look like me, back. Since the game dictates that no one learns to beat the system, my triumphs are met with adversity, mocking, and criticism. This is not true for a white man who made similar decisions and life choices.

Armed with the knowledge my dad gave me, I began my own version of the hustle. Many people think when you say 'street entrepreneur', that means you're a drug dealer. Wrong. I sold many services at the street level (as you will find out later in this chapter), but the image with which the media tried to portray me was utterly false. I was never a drug dealer. The closest I'd been to that life of crime was money laundering, and at that time, I was unaware of the criminal risks of my involvement. Many of the older guys around me were doing the same thing, so it appeared to be legit. At the time, at least, I didn't think the stakes were high on my end. The drug dealers I worked with were just like any other investors or businessmen. They dressed nicely, most were very humble, and none of them seemed anything like the 'villains' portrayed on TV. They had families and businesses, and they wanted what was best for their families, just like everyone else I knew. They may have done some bad things, but with me, it was all business. As their agent, I was buying and setting up businesses—from car washes and barbershops, to night clubs, adult book stores and recording studios. Once I got them set up, I marketed and promoted the businesses. I provided business development and marketing services to a niche clientele base.

By this time, I had met my son's mother who gave birth to Devin Jr., in October of 2002. I had made a name for myself in a short time, just like my father. The only difference between my father and me was that I was around to be there for my son. For a while, life was going well, but life on the streets is very fragile and volatile. There's no such thing as sustainability in that kind of environment. Every day is a risk, and you're lucky if you make it out alive or don't spend your life in prison. For me, it wasn't too long before I got my biggest life lesson in crisis management, and it would change my life -- and everyone's life around me -- forever.

MY DARK (BUT NOT SECRET) PAST

Even though I was a hustler, I knew that one day I would need to find a way to make it out of the ghetto. I believe that we often miss the true meaning of the word "ghetto." The ghetto is not a geographic location, but a state of mind, constructed to keep marginalized members of society oppressed. I was determined to eventually leave this mental state, and progress into true enlightenment.

I had enrolled in Southwest Tennessee Community College (STCC) but, like most students, I was indecisive about majors. I possessed only my enthusiasm about learning how the mind works and my love for working with equipment. My professors and counselors took notice and recommended that I look into the biomedical field. Shortly thereafter, I received a research scholarship through both Southwest Tennessee Community College and the University of Tennessee, in partnership with the National Institute of Health's Bridge Program. The program offered me an opportunity to work with Dr. Paul Herron, one of the area's most distinguished black neuroscientists. Dr. Herron was the first African-American male scholar I had ever spent time with, and he left a lasting impression on me. He never allowed me to complain about my circumstances. Whenever I had an outside issue, he told me to "leave that outside of the lab." His impression on my life, particularly regarding the separation of one's professional and personal life, provided me with invaluable work attributes that would prove themselves useful later in life.

My research with Dr. Herron provided me a fantastic opportunity to reach outside of my comfort zone. In 2002, I served as the oral presenter for Dr. Paul Herron and the Health Bridge Program at the Annual Biomedical Research Conference for Minority Students in New Orleans. I presented research Dr. Herron, others and I had conducted to determine the loss of ACh on GAD (Glutamic acid decarboxylase, a synthetic enzyme for GABA), synaptic proteins, synaptophysin, N-methyl-D-aspartate (NMDA) receptors, and Calmodulin-dependent protein kinase II (CAMKII).

Back in my neighborhood, I worked part-time at an adult bookstore on Brooks Road, next door to the infamous late night staple, Pure Passion. The experience helped me to learn things like inventory and daily cash flow figures for the other businesses I had set up. I also worked at a parking garage in downtown Memphis a few nights a week, mostly for major events.

I was on the fast tract, so I did tons of independent study classes. Fast forward—less than one calendar year after I graduated from STCC summa cum laude, while maintaining my Dean's list status, I transferred my credits to the University of Memphis and was pursuing a bachelor's degree.

On Tuesday, February 17th, 2004, I was working in the adult bookstore on Brooks Road. What happened that morning served as a serious turning point in my life. The experience left seemingly insurmountable obstacles in my way, with emotional and physical scars to match. I was never the same after the incident, and if I hadn't been raised in the streets, I could have lost my life.

On that morning, I was counting large bills in my office at the bookstore. I had been up all night with my friends at Pure Passion, and I wasn't in the mood for much else. Nevertheless, because I am a hard worker, I came to work to get the job done. I hit a line of cocaine to get me straight, wiped the powder off my nose, and I heard an unexpected sound at the door. "Gimme the money!" someone shouted.

I realized that I was being robbed. I was ten days away from my 22nd birthday, and in my last year at the University of Memphis.

The intruder entered the store and gained immediate access to my office, which signaled a red flag to me. From my experience, it seemed that he was essentially let into the building. I figured that he had either been there before or was told how to get in. He arrived just before the armored truck was slated to pick up money from the bookstore, which is the only time that the safe is open.

I quickly surveyed him. The man was about 6'2", and at least 195 pounds. I am 5'10, and weighed about 170 at the time. He was wearing all black, with a mask on his face that covered everything but his eyes. I recognized a north Memphis accent immediately.

I was stunned. I wasn't scared—my past run-ins with violence threw fear out of the window. Thankfully, those experiences taught me how to stay calm during a crisis. The only emotion I felt at the time was shock. I was taken aback because my assistant and I were the only ones who knew when the safe was open. The safe was time-locked.

I immediately realized that I had been set up. The money on the counter was from the store, and the black bag in the corner was my life, in stacks of one hundred dollar bills.

The intruder stuck the barrel of the gun in my face. I looked at the small stack of $20 bills and single dollar bills on the counter. I knew that wasn't what he came for, but I just couldn't figure out how he knew his surroundings so well. Either way, I wasn't in the mood for any of his bullshit. I asked, "Do you know who I represent? Do you really want to do this?"

"Gimme the fucking money!" he said. He moved the gun from my face to my chest.

I took a second to weigh my options. This dude seemed like he wasn't the sharpest tool in the shed. I figured he might not be smart enough to realize whose money he was dealing with, which meant that he might actually pull the trigger. Plus, the office only had one way in and one way out. I either had to fight or die. I couldn't run and hide, although a part of me wished there was an option.

With a deep breath, I sighed and said, "Whatever, man. Have fun trying to stay alive." After counting the money, he knew I didn't give him what he came for. When I saw his eyes turn for a split second, my instinct kicked in. I took my chance and knocked the pistol away from my chest and wrestled him to the floor. If he got away with the money he came for I would be dead anyway. There's no BBB (Better Business Bureau) to file a complaint to, no Equifax or Dun's reporting on your debt—you can't owe that kind of money on the streets and stay alive. I pinned him to the ground and began to strike his face repeatedly with something, I can't even remember what I hit him with. I was actually getting the best of him. Then, he and I wrestled to get the gun again and...

BANG!

I couldn't make sense of any of it. My head started swimming, then buzzing, and then I held on, as I experienced what felt like a thousand knives in my left shoulder. It felt like my arm was missing. I started feeling very weak, and before long, I kept remembering that I couldn't relax or close my eyes. I remembered that sleep is the cousin of death, and often serves as a transition to the other side. I fought to stay awake with everything I had.

I was wearing a white dress shirt and tan slacks. I crawled on the floor, watching myself in the mirror as my entire outfit turned a bloody, horrific red. It was, truly, the worst moment of my life. Since I worked in a lab with several rodents and other animals, I didn't vomit at the sight of blood and flesh being scattered everywhere. I did what I could to give myself a makeshift tourniquet and apply pressure. I was still trying to process the fact that this blood was *mine.*

I fought for my life the way I always had. I couldn't stand up due to having a gaping hole in my upper extremity and loss of blood and balance. I couldn't hear because the blast was so close to my head; I was losing blood fast, my clothes were soaked in blood, and blood was all over the room. I just barely made it to my phone, and I yelled for my assistant while crawling on the ground. My assistant was in shock, looking at me dying on the floor, and wasn't able to call 911. I had to do it myself. Eventually the medics came, and I was taken away on a stretcher.

The police came to the scene, and before long, conducted an investigation. Now, I know I'm responsible for being involved in a shady business. But for all the "looking" into the business, not one minute of police time was spent investigating the man who robbed and shot me or (nor) the people who sent him. Not one minute. To the police, the act was simply another black on black crime. When an individual is not participating in the system, you can't even call the police and get them to do their jobs.

As a black man from the inner city, seeing a policeman incited an inherent sense of fear within myself. Police are the enemy to my people. I didn't have social media or the Internet growing up, but I still saw many examples of police misconduct and brutality for most of my life. My entire community shares that fear. What made me loathe policemen, however, happened in the aftermath of my shooting. There was no follow-up, no investigation into my shooting. This very experience mirrors what blacks across the country go through in their own neighborhoods. The police routinely disconnect from the black community's instances of mistreatment and crime, but are 'tasked' to 'protect' the very neighborhoods that they so blatantly ignore. How is it that the drug dealers and gang leaders I worked with could use their resources to identify the gunman who had attempted to steal their cash and take my life, but the police couldn't?

Police fail to realize that the incidents that happen in one city shape community experiences for black men and minorities everywhere. In my company, one team member has labeled this phenomenon as "Police as a Brand." This fosters a universal fear of policemen within the black community. As black men, we fear that we are not only targeted by police as perpetrators, but are utterly disrespected/disregarded by them when we're victims, and are unjustly convicted by both the public and the media if anyone dares to speak in our defense.

It took months for me to get back on my feet. I would never truly recover from that injury and was left with scars and dysfunction to my left arm that will be with me for the rest of my life. I was left with a permanent disability in my left shoulder, and serious damage to my axillary nerve.

I eventually had internal fixation in my left shoulder, with an intramedullary nail and locking screws, two of which were placed proximally near my shoulder and two of which were placed in the distal humerus from an anterior approach. I was born ambidextrous—I played bass guitar, drums and piano, and even played sports with interchangeable hand control—but I was left-hand dominant. People make jokes about not being able to read my handwriting, but I had to learn how to write again, and I still have no feeling in nearly half of my left hand. I was forced to drop out of college just short of graduation, which meant I had nothing to look forward to in terms of post-grad employment. But, for the sake of my son and his mother, I was determined to keep standing. After being shot, I hated returning to the street life. The damages were tangible, and the risks were finally real to me. Before the shooting, it never occurred to me that I would ever stare death in the face. It happened around me frequently to others, but I never thought it would happen to me. I was wrong.

On October 20, 2004 about 3:00 p.m., I again stared death in the face. I was working on some campaign materials for a political candidate when my home, my family, and my own life were threatened. I was involved in a near-fatal home invasion less than six months after recovering from a near fatal robbery and shooting myself. Two men came into my East

Memphis home, at 3202 Clearbrook and one of them held out a nine-millimeter handgun, told me to lie down, and told me that he was going to rob me. I immediately ran to grab my own gun. Once the intruders saw that I had a gun, they ran. As I chased them out of my home one of the men proceeded to shoot. I shot back and killed one of the intruders.

At the time of the home invasion, I was still recovering from my injury from the previous shooting only 6 months back in February. The shooting left me with a grueling rehabilitation schedule, and a lowered ability to protect my family from the lifestyle I left behind. I could barely walk. I was on five different pain medications, and I was having difficulty relieving myself due to meds so I had a catheter in my penis. Needless to say, I defended my home as best I could, and I survived.

When the cops showed up to my house and saw the scene, they didn't care about any of the surrounding evidence. They loosely questioned some neighbors, who reiterated that there was a lot of suspicious activity around my house that day, but included only partial statements that made it next to impossible for anyone to see the crime scene the way it looked when things took place. For example, they did not investigate the following:

Rodney Steward, "victim," was a known drug dealer and gangster disciple. His girlfriend, Tamiko Jackson, affirmed that he was a drug dealer in her witness statement, and evidence showed he had crack cocaine on him at the time of his death and his toxicology report was negative for crack cocaine.

A female and male witness reported a white SUV (2000 white Ford Expedition) and a black car (99 Nissan) drive

south down Clearbrook and turn around driving North toward Knight Arnold. The female witness reported hearing
shots fired after seeing the vehicles make their way back
down the street.

Lafaro Jeffries (homicide suspect) was pulled over and
taken into custody for having gun powder residue on his
hands while driving an SUV (2000 white Ford Expedition).
He claimed he didn't leave his job at Family First Mortgage
until 3:30p.m., and listed his boss as "Carlos Hobson" as an
alibi. However, according to a fax received on 05/20/2005
sent to the Criminal Court Clerks Office by the real Carlos B.
Hobson of Family First Mortgage,

> "As to Lafaro Jeffries. Does not work for Family First Mort-
> gage. He has never been an employee of Family First
> Mortgage."

The black car described by myself, the male witness, and
the female witness also matches the description of the "victims" best friend's car.

An anonymous caller gave a witness statement that she
saw a 2003 Alero Oldsmobile 2 door leaving the scene of the
incident and come back and park near the officer's cars.

Note: Tamika Steward (sister of "victim") owned a silver
2 door Oldsmobile Alero. She also claimed to have been at
work all day and nobody drove her car.

Later in an interview with police, when confronted about
her car being parked near the scene of the crime, she stated
once she heard of the incident her boss let her leave work
and said she didn't have to clock out.

A female officer was in the crowd at the crime scene when
she noticed another neighbor walk from behind his home,
(which was behind mine), with a silver object she thought

was a gun and said she saw a male running to the back yards carrying something. The female officer stated the following: "I saw someone walking to his porch with his left hand under his shirt, as he stepped up on his porch; I could see silver and I'm assuming it was a weapon; all I saw was silver metal. I stepped out from my doorway so he could see me and he looked startled and went into his house."

On a phone call to the Homicide Office, Room 11-21, 201 Poplar in Memphis on Wednesday, October 20, 2004 at 1535 hours the female officer stated that she did not want to be involved because the boys on her street are Gangster Disciples and she advised MPD that the person she saw was also a Gangster Disciple.

They glossed over the evidence, picking up "pieces" of the story, while missing many of the important details that that would have helped to re-enact the occurrences, in the same way that the media uses sound bites to summarize a story. The problem is that no one really knows what happened, and since the police are the authority and I am just a black man, the police get to decide the narrative.

The police never care about what happens to black men, and neither does society. Unfortunately, it's our shared reality. I wasn't handcuffed on the ride downtown, but I was taken into custody and placed on a 72-hour hold, pending investigation. If I was such a threat, why wasn't I handcuffed immediately? If it was clear that I shot and killed an "unarmed man," why wasn't I charged immediately?

While I was downtown, the police issued a warrant to search my house. When the evidence was processed, the police claimed they couldn't find any bullet casings or shells from anyone's gun but mine. So when my 72-hour hold was up, I was held on a 48-hour hold and charged with first degree murder. Instead of looking for the men who were contracted to kill my family, and me, the police tore up my house looking for drugs and money. They didn't find any drugs, because there weren't any to be found. It felt like the entire scene was flipped to make me the aggressor. I had never been the aggressor. I had no criminal record, no known enemies, and no reason to want to kill anyone or put my family and myself in that situation. I firmly believe that I was framed. We spent months in court, and did what we could to get all the evidence to surface. I went through numerous attorneys who all suggested I take a plea deal before they even knew all the details of my case. It was like the attorneys weren't interested in fighting for me because my case was assigned to Judge Chris Craft, who had a reputation in the streets for railroading black men, similar to Judge Brockmeyer in Ferguson. One of my former clients, who ran one of the largest drug distribution networks in the city, told me there was only one attorney I should trust to represent me. He recommended a successful criminal attorney named Gerald Skahan who, after I met with him, agreed to take my case. But in the end, we still weren't able to find all the evidence from the crime scene to exonerate me.

After nearly four years of battling in the courts, I was convicted of reckless homicide, but I hadn't been convicted based on what really happened, so I continued to fight and appealed the conviction. I hadn't given up ever in my life so I wasn't going to start giving up here. I leveraged everything I had on the appeal and ultimately went bankrupt, losing all my possessions, including my home. I bet it all because a felony meant my life was over. And I lost. What guilty man, cold-blooded killer like they tried to paint me, would be angry about receiving a sentence of 90 days in jail and five years of probation? In the streets that is winning, but I was innocent, so anything other than a justifiable homicide, given all I had been through, was unacceptable.

After I lost the appeal and faced homelessness again, I faced the fact that I would be labeled a felon for the rest of my life. My education, and everything I had been working on, was taken away. In an instant, I couldn't rent a place, I couldn't get a loan, and I couldn't win a contract. I couldn't go get a job if I wanted to, and was denied my disability claim for social security because I was "young enough" to work through my disability. I couldn't get public assistance either. Any future plans for a legitimate life were taken away, and I was denied diversion, an opportunity to forego criminal charges and a criminal record. I was stripped of all my possible career options that would position me to be able to care for my family; how could I be seen as a man if I couldn't take care of my fatherly responsibilities? I felt that I could never move on and that again I had let my loved ones down. My back was against the wall and this had to be one of the scariest times in my life—but it was nothing I couldn't handle. The odds had been against me my whole life.

At the time of the incident in 2004, I was renting the house in East Memphis with my family, trying to build a life for myself, after leaving the streets. At this time my son was in diapers. Because of the first shooting in February at the store, I had to switch things up and focus solely on my creativity. I have loved music since childhood. All of my siblings and I were musically gifted, and I was also lyrically and artistically gifted. I could do graphic design, I produced my own tracks, wrote books and poems, played bass guitar, and wrote raps that quickly earned the respect of some local DJs and others, as I hustled on the streets, selling CDs to support my family.

I made numerous underground mix tapes and original albums under the stage name Nez P, and appeared at shows throughout the southern part of the United States. Some of my former rap hustlers are now very successful in the music business, and will always be like family. Eventually, my small artwork projects began to pay off, so I started my graphic design business. I named it Native Graphix, and promoted it as 'a one stop shop for all your creative needs'.

I started Native Graphix out of necessity and disability. I needed something that I could do with the click of a mouse because the rehabilitation from the shooting was intense. I only had one arm to work with, so, during this time, I had to learn to use my non-dominant hand, or my ability to earn a living was over. It was the ultimate reinvention—with my new business, I evolved from a street entrepreneur to a rising creative strategist, and many local business owners and political figures (from state representatives and congressional candidates to judges in Memphis) were calling me to develop their campaign artwork and materials.

So, contrary to what the courts and the media have led the public to believe about me, I didn't shoot an unarmed man. I didn't shoot someone who was knocking on my door for help. I was setup. My story hasn't changed since that day because it's the truth. You can read the transcripts of my testimony on public record—that way, you can know the whole story. The media decided to frame its saga of stories based solely on the keywords 'reckless homicide', the charge that I was convicted of as a result of the home invasion. This is a narrative that does not include statements from witnesses regarding suspicious activity, or inconsistencies in anyone else's alibi involved with the intruders (known in this case as the victim's) entourage.

The media and police ignored all the positives in my life and only portrayed me as a rapper to attach a negative connotation to the story. They posted my mugshot and immediately excluded any information about my being a first time offender, a model student, a college senior, and a responsible father. It was a complete character assassination. I was almost killed, and just like Mike Brown, they set it up to look like it was my fault.

> *"Just because something isn't a lie does not mean that it isn't deceptive. A liar knows that he is a liar, but one who speaks mere portions of truth in order to deceive is a craftsmen of destruction"*
>
> *– Criss Jami*

I have struggled through immense tragedy and pain at the hands of the justice system – I am just thankful that I, as a black man, am living to tell others my story. I shared the stories from my life because I wanted to make one thing clear. From my dark past and troubled upbringing, to my life as a businessman today, I am still living with the fear and disdain for the police and the system that was instilled in me as a small child, and further reinforced in me, from a very young age. One of my brothers is in law enforcement, so I am not a person that has that infamous, NWA-originated "Fuck the Police" mentality. At this point, however, it's delusional to think that the African-American community is not justified in its fear of the system and its law enforcement officials. My people are completely justified, and I am no exception. I still fear the law to this day-- whether it comes in the form of a badge or a court system-- because of the abuses that have been practiced upon me.

> Daily the Negro is coming more and more to look upon law and justice, not as protecting safeguards, but as sources of humiliation and oppression. The laws are made by men who have little interest in him, they are executed by men who have absolutely no motive for treating the black people with courtesy or consideration; and, finally, the accused law-breaker is tried, not by his peers but often by men who would rather punish ten innocent Negroes than let one guilty one escape.
>
> – W.E.B. Dubois

When the shooting in Ferguson occurred, many officers were seen in the media wearing bracelets with the phrase, "I am Darren Wilson." It was meant to show unity in their support for their co-worker who had killed Michael Brown. And since I was often seen together with officers and other officials from the City of Ferguson, people naturally assumed that I supported, or even took part in, the "I am Darren Wilson" campaign. Obviously, I am not Darren Wilson. I am a black man, raised by a black family, fighting against the system built to destroy black America. I am a man who rose from the bottom, who lacked the necessary role models to help steer me in the right direction. I am one of the millions of black men who have been racially profiled and wrongfully targeted by police, mistreated by the courts, and portrayed unfairly by the media. I am a walking miracle, an inspiration, a story, and a journey.

I am Mike Brown.

WHY IT MATTERS

I was chastised for being an "Oreo," a black man with a white mentality, by members of the black community who didn't know I could relate to their struggles. While I was in Ferguson, I was the only person in the room who knew what they were going through. This epithet immediately attached to my public persona, even though I grew up in a poverty-stricken area and had lived near, and worked in, Ferguson for nearly seven years. I felt insulted for even needing to explain that I can relate to people who had experienced many of the same hardships I faced throughout my entire life.

When most people think of my life, they think of the single fact that my firm and I were publicly fired because of my felony, and the media stories about my background and the unfair comparison they tried to make between Darren Wilson and me. However, people fail to realize that I was vilified by the very same system that we all believe allowed Wilson to walk home free, yet vilified Brown himself. The media perpetually syndicated that narrative to keep me from leading change within a system filled with institutional racism.

In the early Ferguson meetings, we talked about my dark past and how I had fought my way to where I am today. We talked about my experience growing up in abject poverty, a broken household, and no working utilities; how I was racially profiled even before I started stealing to feed my family as a little boy. We talked about my experience being spit on by white people and other whites locking their car doors when I walked past (I still experience that today). I was contracted with the Economic Partnership, so, how could we not talk about how I struggled to make ends meet, grew up on food stamps and how the low-end job market traps underserved communities? My whole life was like a case study to the partnership, St. Louis County and Ferguson officials, on the benefits of "entrepreneurship and innovation" for underserved communities. There was never a question as to whether or not I could advise Ferguson city officials on how to improve relations with the black community that they were trying to engage, and there was never any truth to the rumor that we were fired due to my felony.

I was fired because I was the only one among the St. Louis Economic Development Partnership's (the Partnership) leadership who was actually working for the benefit of the black community in Ferguson, and not for my own personal interest. So, despite being perfectly aware of my background and my felony (and despite its being one of the reasons my firm was contracted in the first place), the partnership decided to leak my background to the media with a negative spin rather than telling the positive story of overcoming odds we discussed so many times in the past. Although my conviction was already a part of public record, I was on the verge of uncovering the veil and uniting the black community throughout the county, and the partnership didn't want that. To distract and further divide the black community, they extracted specific quotes that detailed specifics about my case to paint me as a "killer"; that way, they could convince the public that we had no shared experiences and all the negative stories they would pen about me were all credible.

I admit that I have made many mistakes in my short time here on this earth, but I am not what I went through and I'm not living the rest of my life in my past. I realize that my life matters, all lives matter, especially the lives of my people, black people, all over this world. The media tirade set up against me taught me a valuable lesson: that the media, Missouri and St. Louis government did not have any regard for my life.

The emotional stress of the situation was both unnecessary and unduly painful. I was only attempting to bring everyone together to effect real change. In turn, I got nothing. In the height of the "Black Lives Matter" campaign, St. Louis media and officials gave me a crash course in the opposite.

Both the Partnership and many of the St. Louis City and County officials never saw Michael Brown's death as a tragedy. They only saw it as a threat to business revenues, and their solution was cover ups and high-level marketing campaigns to distract the public. This is nothing new, however— only one of the latest additions in a history of abuse, misuse, corruption, institutional bias, and racism.

We see the level of abuse and corruption exhibited by both the Partnership and Ferguson officials in many St. Louis government organizations—from the police department to prisons. Reddit Hudson, a former St. Louis police officer, stated that many of his peers at the St. Louis Police Department were "deeply racist," and that "officers saw young black and brown men as targets. They would respond with force to even minor offenses."[3] Reddit claims that he was "floored by the dysfunctional culture [he] encountered" when he joined the police department in 1994. Hudson also authored the 2009 American Civil Liberties Union (ACLU)

---

[3] "Being a Cop Showed Me Just How Racist and Violent the Police Are. There's Only One Fix." *Washington Post*. The Washington Post, 6 Dec. 2014. Web. 14 May 2015.

report entitled "Suffering in Silence: Human Rights Abuses in St. Louis Correctional Centers." "Suffering in Silence" is a summary of the ACLU's 2007 investigation into the St. Louis penal system. The findings of the report were astonishing. The ACLU cited repeated incidences of "systemic cover-up[s] of incidents," "false reporting," "negligence resulting in death," "intimidation," and failed oversight" by the Department of Public Safety, as well as many other abuses in the St. Louis penal system. In the report, the ACLU revealed that "a culture of abuse is encouraged inside the [correctional centers] and those [correctional officers] who adapt themselves to it and embrace the systemic cover-up of the abuse are advantaged with promotions or other favors from administrators."[4] Even in 2015, we see these attitudes ingrained in the minds of St. Louis-area police departments, adding even more weight to the argument alleging a long history of police abuse as one of the reasons for the divide between black residents and police officers in St. Louis and St. Louis County alike.

Perhaps the most obvious form of institutionalized discrimination within St. Louis and St. Louis County lies within its ticketing system. In 2013, St. Louis City and County courts collected more than $61 million in traffic fines and fees.[5] Better Together STL's report on the municipal court system, entitled Public Safety – Municipal Courts, examines and verifies racial and economically based disparities in St.

[4] Author: Reddit Hudson. Http://www.aclu-mo.org/files/7213/4255/6443/ACLUSufferingFullReport.pdf (n.d.): n. pag. Suffering in Silence: Human Rights Abuses in St. Louis Correctional Centers. American Civil Liberties Union, 2009. Web. 15 May 2015.

[5] Author: Better Together STL. http://www.bettertogetherstl.com/wp-content/uploads/2014/10/BT-Municipal-Courts-Report-Full-Report1.pdf. Public Safety -- Municipal Courts. Better Together STL, 2014. Web. 22 June 2015.

Louis and St. Louis County communities. The article states that "many of the municipal courts in St. Louis County have lost the trust of their communities, especially those in which residents are predominantly African-American and poor." Additionally, the report states that municipal courts "often go to extreme measures in order to collect fines and fees... [including] locking up citizens without the means to pay their fines, and warrants to those who do not appear (often out of fear that their inability to pay will result in them being locked up)." The discrimination is even recognized at the state level. The Missouri Attorney General's "Executive Summary for 2013 Missouri Vehicle Stops" reveals that black drivers were 66 percent more likely than white drivers to be stopped.6 The overwhelming evidence shows the disproportionate nature of how African-Americans are treated in St. Louis. An even more disturbing fact is that no one seems to care. These systems have been in place for years, and as more time passes, more humiliating secrets are buried under the surface. When working in Ferguson, I was given a glimpse of the cover-ups and schemes required to perpetuate these types of attitudes.

I'm here to expose all of the lies, with the evidence I have. The institutional racism that came to a head in Ferguson is still alive and thriving in poor black neighborhoods across the country. The fire set by institutional racism is blazing and burning, torturing every black soul who lives within America's borders. As we see more violent protests in other American cities like Baltimore, Maryland, it is imperative for us to realize the swelling anger and fatigue in black communities. We are tired of the racism. We are tired of police

6 "2013 VEHICLE STOPS EXECUTIVE SUMMARY." *2013 Executive Summary.* Missouri Attorney General, n.d. Web. 25 June 2015.

monitoring. We are tired of the stereotypes. These instances represent the fire, and the fire will never be put out unless "white America" admits its existence and takes steps to correct the issues.

My story, and my unraveling of the corruption, began only a few days before August 9, 2014, that fateful day in Ferguson when Michael Brown was murdered.

CHAPTER 2

NORTH ST. LOUIS COUNTY (NSTLC)

LONG BEFORE AUGUST

FERGUSON IS A SMALL CITY, with a population of approximately 21,200. Of those 21,200 residents, about 15,000 are black. Many of Ferguson's inhabitants are poor. The town's unemployment rate has ballooned from less than five percent in 2000 to over thirteen percent in 2010-12.[7] About one in four residents lives below the poverty line, with an

---

[7] Von Hoffman, Constantine. "Hit by Poverty, Ferguson Reflects the New Suburbs." *CBSNews*. CBS Interactive, 19 Aug. 2014. Web. 26 June 2015.

income per capital of around $21,000. [8] Although Ferguson's residents are predominately black, both the local government and the police force are run almost entirely by white staff. When considering the inherently racist nature of St. Louis County government, this dynamic only added fuel to the fire during the Mike Brown tragedy.

In contrast to media reports, I was never hired directly by the city to handle media or perform public relations services. My firm was contracted to develop an outreach and engagement strategy to repair bridges between the city and the African-American community. That story began with the local media in Saint Louis. Interestingly, one would think the local media outlets would be the most vested in the integrity of the local story, but I've learned differently. The media works around soundbites. They don't have time in their news segment to cover the detailed story, so they extract the juiciest parts and go for ratings.

However, some of the reporters who broke the story of my past had to know that it was a lie. This is because they were friends with the owners of Elasticity and Common Ground, who were "actually" handling media and public relations for Ferguson. It was a blatant lie, told in order to paint a negative picture of me and attribute all the negative press to me. Consequently, their lies made me appear noncredible, and made my strategy for the black community seem ineffective.

People in the community, including those listening and watching around the world, automatically assumed that my role was as the media stated, and didn't bother to fact check.

---

[8] Von Hoffman, Constantine. "Hit by Poverty, Ferguson Reflects the New Suburbs." *CBSNews*. CBS Interactive, 19 Aug. 2014. Web. 26 June 2015.

Once the story leaked onto national and international media, it became a prime example of a case of the old saying, "if you lie enough times, it eventually becomes truth".

I never worked for Ferguson directly in the beginning. In fact, my role began at the county level before the tragedy of Michael Brown ever took place.

My team began working in North County on February 26, 2014. I was sent an RFP (Request for Proposal) via e-mail to bid on a work assignment by Katherine "Katy" Jamboretz, the contract administrator who manages all the marketing contracts for the Partnership. My firm submitted a bid, and Katy suggested we partner with Elasticity, an all-white, male-owned marketing firm that gets tons of contracts from the partnership.

Our first meeting regarding the North County work was on Monday, April 14, 2014 at the Partnership's headquarters in Clayton. The meeting took place in Board Room 2346, the room where most of the Ferguson strategy meetings would take place. It is important to note that co-owner Aaron Perlut is a friend of Katy's; when Aaron has an idea, Katy finds a way to get it funded. Their bond made them partners in the nonsensical strategies that were presented by Aaron and his firm.

Because the Partnership was the driving economic force in the region, the power lies with them. They can assemble meetings with all influential individuals from the state's largest corporations whenever they need them. The few blacks there with a seat at the table were what most would call token blacks, such as Rodney Crim (President of the Partnership), and Jackie Wellington (Vice-President). They

worked directly with then African American County Executive, Charlie Dooley. The three of them exhibited an attitude
that proved detrimental to progress in the African-American
community—they collectively endorse projects that continually and disproportionately trap and punish African
Americans.

When Michael Brown was killed, no one in state leadership knew what to do (or if they did, you couldn't tell). Each
day brought a new set of blunders from various government
offices, from the Governor's office all the way to Ferguson's
City Hall. I can't even count the number of meetings I was in
where I suggested that the Governor fire his writers and staff
for setting him up for failure. One would think that the Governor's strategy team would have a better grasp on
positioning him (to) display some type of cultural competency. What is culture? Culture is the sum of a group's religion,
values, art and music, patterns of behavior or social habits,
language, cuisine, and so on. What is cultural competence?
Cultural competence is being able to effectively interact with
people who are different and when all of the before-
mentioned characteristics are different from yours.

There are many levels to cultural competence, and even
though Katy and Aaron have issues understanding other
cultures, they were nowhere near as bad as Governor Nixon.
Katy, Aaron and I would cringe anytime he took the stage,
due to his almost always off-based speeches and delivery
when it came to the issues in Ferguson or the black community. He was also unnecessarily awkward around black
people who weren't elected officials, and struggled with relating to black residents.

While the state and county pontificated, the Partnership
offered to cover the fees of a couple of public relations firms

that were considered to be the best in both the St. Louis area and statewide. The Partnership chose Elasticity and Common Ground Public Relations, which was named by Small Business Monthly one of the "Best Public Relations Firms" in both 2013 and 2014. [9]

Before the incident, the Partnership's role was to stimulate economic growth in St. Louis County through real estate expansion, innovation and job creation. There was a major problem, however, that came to light after a short time under contract with the Partnership. The problem, as many noted, was that St. Louis County had a largely African-American population, and for decades they had been neglected in every way. This was by design. So how could the Partnership possibly relate to a black community after years of abuse? Why would the black community trust the Partnership to make decisions about what's best for them without truly engaging in a dialogue? A true dialogue.

> *Leaders who do not act dialogically, but insist on imposing their decisions, do not organize the people--they manipulate them. They do not liberate, nor are they liberated: they oppress.*
> *-- Paolo Freire*

The short answer is that they couldn't. Even if they tried would the black community have been receptive?

The next lie that has effectively "become true" through the magical workings of the local media is the notion that I was an outsider from Memphis who was called in to save the day.

---

[9] *Awards.* Small Business Monthly. Webpage can be found here: http://www.sbmon.com/Awards?Search=common+ground

In reality, the Devin James Group had already been an established and respected firm in St. Louis for quite some time. I was hailed by many publications as a positive force for the community. I was even called a St. Louis native in an article from *The St. Louis American*, the main African-American newspaper in St. Louis, when I completed an accelerated business course at the University of Washington's Foster School of Business, for which I was elected class president. For someone to assert that I "flew in" and was unaffiliated with local leaders and the community, or to insinuate I was not respected throughout the State of Missouri is a flagrant lie. My firm and I had been there for years, and had both the clients and testimonials to back it up.

The Partnership knew all of this. In fact, they had lauded my work in the region. The CEO of the Partnership at the time, Denny Coleman, commended me for overcoming my rough past. I was also recommended to the Partnership by long-time friend Rita Days, a beloved former state senator and minority advocate in the state of Missouri. Charlie Dooley, the first ever African-American County Executive for St. Louis County, endorsed me. I had supported both Charlie and Rita and contributed efforts to Dooley's previous campaigns in the past. It was an honor to have two elite African-Americans in the St. Louis community support me.

Before August 9th, my firm was tasked to perform a brand assessment to determine how we could effectively market the region. We had to get feedback from the community, specifically, the black community in the area. Although our firm had already done work in St. Louis for prior contracts, this contract was unique because it was an election year for Dooley. As such, we were implicitly tasked with "making him look good."

Dooley was down in the polls, and it was almost certain he would lose his seat. Phase 1 of our contract was all about going into the community with more of a grassroots approach, talking to everyday citizens, and getting a grasp of their perspectives on North St. Louis County as related to overall attitude, morale, pride, community participation, and more. While my team handled the heavy lifting in the community, Elasticity and one of their subcontractors were conducting electronic surveys aimed to reflect both internal and external residents, in and around the county, with hundreds of questions about their opinions of North St. Louis County.

When our collective research was finished, the Partnership complimented our assertive approach. "Great!" Partnership members said. "When can we have it?"

Our team had already been in the community for weeks, interviewing everyone from homeless teens to business executives, inside and outside of North County. I remember being at the Town Hall Meeting for the closing of Jamestown Mall on July 21, 2014. Dooley and his spokesperson, Patricia Washington, were there, and were having a rough time with the crowd. The distorted sound system made matters worse. The black community was the most vocal about their issues, but all residents in attendance complained about the decline of the area and their property values. Dooley looked dumbfounded the entire meeting and received mixed reviews, and even a few "fuck you's" after the meeting.

According to Elasticity's proposal, "Bridging the challenges faced in NSTLC are more easily stated than remedied. There is a vast array of both perceptual and very real challenges facing NSTLC, and any program aimed at revitalizing economic development therein will first require a change in mindset both amongst those who live and work there, and those who look at the area from afar." I immediately saw the issues within that statement. The people who live and work in North St. Louis County are not the ones who needed to change. Their government needed, and still needs, to change. Elasticity and their subcontractor were relying primarily on web-based digital survey data (think Survey Monkey) to do its research. My issues were simple: the majority of people in the underserved communities may not have the time to spare or tools, like a computer and internet access, to complete an electronic survey. This means that the most vulnerable population, the entire focus of this effort, couldn't be reached, and their input wouldn't be included. This thwarted the entire purpose of our work. If our voices don't matter, I'd rather government be honest. We don't need to feel like our voice matters if it doesn't.

Additionally, the surveys were flawed because the website to access the survey doesn't authenticate users or recognize when an IP address has been used more than once. Those who access the link can complete a survey, and they can do that as many times as they want. As such, there is no way to authenticate the results. Governments do this often to falsely justify spending. I wouldn't be surprised if the entire budget for the partnership was based on bogus research that created "a need."

The Partnership was desperately trying to make this research look authentic. The in-depth interviews conducted by Elasticity and their subcontractor were also rigged, using only internal and external stakeholders that both Katy and Aaron selected to 'control' the responses. Aren't these the same people who hired me because they didn't understand, and couldn't relate, to the black community? If so, then why were they appropriating funds and assignments for projects and overseeing the research that would impact this very group?

My firm's goal was to present our research and findings on August 13, 2014. We didn't have any clue how important our findings would be in the coming days. Elasticity and their subcontractor were not really open to including "real" perspectives at all. After all, the perspectives I had were all extremely negative, raw and to the point. When my team presented our findings to our partner firms, we were essentially told not to worry about it and that their teams could handle it. This presented a red flag to me because I knew, again, that the black community's voice would not be heard.

By the beginning of August, Elasticity and their subcontractor had completed the research that they would pose as "our" county research, and compiled a 36-page document that laid out the empirical data. Here, for the public, were the findings in the truncated version of the research:

Q: Generally speaking, do you feel things in North St. Louis County are moving in the right or wrong direction?

North County Residents:	
Right Direction (Strongly):	1%
Right Direction (Somewhat):	33%
Unsure:	18%
Wrong Direction (Somewhat):	31%
Wrong Direction (Strongly):	16%

External Residents:	
Right Direction (Strongly):	1%
Right Direction (Somewhat):	20%
Unsure:	30%
Wrong Direction (Somewhat):	32%
Wrong Direction (Strongly):	17%

Q: How would you rate the "performance" of North St. Louis County in each of the following areas?

North County Residents:	
Quality of Life	42%
Embracing Diversity	41%
Local Workforce	35%
Safety	33%
Local Economy	27%
Schools and Education	27%

We asked dozens of questions just like this, and polled people of all races. What remained true throughout our statistical analysis was that: a) people from North County had an unfavorable view of their community, and possessed a low sense of community pride; and b) people outside of North County saw North County as a joke, and a place to steer clear of at all costs. In fact, when asked whether they found North County an attractive place to live, only 4% responded "yes." Only 2% said they would even consider moving there if they were looking to move.

Among the recurring pessimism that the data proved to show, we zoned in on a few key talking points in our presentation to the Partnership:

- Internal survey data showed that the general population sees North County as performing poorly, and only 37% agree that "residents are proud of their community." Accounting for these negative viewpoints is critical in a marketing and communications campaign.
- Crime is the driver of negative opinion in North St. Louis County, and needs to be addressed.
- The diverse nature of the area, both ethnic, religious, and socio-economic, is a strength mentioned by almost all residents. Notably, a few respondents only expanded on these strengths; this suggests that talking points need to be developed around this issue.

It is important to note that we were not evaluating racial tension as a primary factor at this time. This was before August 9, and within white St. Louis County, there was little cause for concern on the superficial level. However, there was a deeply embedded level of racial tension among African Americans long before the turn of the century.

Ferguson has been an anomaly in North County for decades. During the civil rights movement, there was a great migration within St. Louis County. As the black population expanded, no true leader ever stepped up in their favor. While there was civil unrest, white leaders could walk all over the residents. No one stepped up to speak for black people in the area.

When the migration occurred, the historically white City of Ferguson started receiving an increased number of African-American residents. The white population was still in charge, however, because all the elected officials and power positions were white. It was no secret that the whites saw their town slipping away, and they did anything they could to stay in power. Today, Ferguson is one of the most disproportionately represented cities in Missouri, with a nearly all-white government representing an African-American majority population.

When I was called into North County to perform the brand assessment before the death of Michael Brown, I was inheriting a mess that went far beyond my own years. At the time of my assignment, I would have said that anything could improve with time, transparency, and understanding. But the coming days would prove me wrong. I was in way over my head, but I was the only one who seemed to have his head on straight.

CHAPTER 3

THE GALVANIZING MOMENT

ON AUGUST 9, 2014, Officer Darren Wilson was driving down Canfield Drive in Ferguson, Missouri. He was in route to a call he had received about a sick infant. He noticed two young black males walking down the middle of a residential road. He pulled his police car up to the young men, now known as Michael Brown and Dorian Johnson, and told them to get off the street. A verbal argument, and later, a physical altercation, occurred. Less than a minute later, Michael Brown was shot and killed in broad daylight.

Even before backup police arrived at the scene, residents began to surround the scene. The media arrived shortly after that, and began distributing the story to the rest of the world.

Before nightfall even came, the City of Ferguson was infamous. Articles, blogs, and social media posts took over the story.

In all of its thoroughness, the media never allowed room for Michael Brown to be viewed as a human being. His death was never humanized, as it should have been. As soon as media outlets received the news, the story was edited for mass media, looped on the negatives, and distributed to the masses. The story was promoted as the "new sensation," and it contributed to waves of chaos during the time. We must remember that the media has a social responsibility to manage the impact of their work on the public. As someone who worked extensively in the field, and has worked with many of the journalists and reporters covering the events surrounding the Mike Brown tragedy, it is my opinion that the media simply failed to gain sight of their responsibility in this matter.

We must always remember that despite the mark that the Michael Brown case left on the world, Michael Brown was just an ordinary kid. At the time of his death, Michael was an 18-year-old young man who had graduated from Normandy High School just days before. He was slated to attend Vatterott College on August 11th, where he planned to learn air conditioning and furnace repair. His family referred to him as a "gentle giant," and he was known for being a kind soul who made others laugh. Michael had dreams of owning his own business. He was the oldest of three children, and was raised by both his mother and father in St. Louis County.

Set aside your opinions. Set aside what you think happened the day of the shooting. None of that matters, because a young man is dead.

When Michael Brown was killed, I posted the following message to Twitter, in a fit of rage from which many thought I should have restrained myself:

> *"Fucking crazy [...] Unarmed teenage boy #killed by #Ferguson #police Y'all better wake up and stop killing..."*

People in my industry told me that I should have toned it down. They were right, in that it was in my best interest from a public relations perspective. But as a black man, a father and a human being, I felt obligated to express myself. My emotions were so high. I saw this young man as myself, because there were so many times when I could have been killed. My life was rough, but I dodged death many times. I was given so many second chances, but Brown was not.

I also saw him as my young son, Devin Jr., who was eleven years old at the time. Devin Jr. was only beginning to learn all of the injustices that the world had to offer him. How would I feel if my own son fell to the same fate as Brown?

I was so enraged by the story that to this day, I do not regret sending out that message. Not one bit. In fact, I'm proud of myself, because I stuck to my convictions. Instead of falling in line with my colleagues, I chose to express my unadulterated frustration that was also being collectively vented by hundreds of thousands of people around the world.

In the ensuing days, the nation would watch, marvel, and even remotely participate, as the story of Michael Brown became about much more than the tragic death of a young man at the hands of a police officer.

On August 10th, the day after the shooting, there was a candlelight vigil held to commemorate Brown. As tensions rose, however, a group of restless citizens lashed out, and the once-peaceful event erupted into a violent outburst. Not far from the scene of the shooting, buildings were ransacked, looted, vandalized and destroyed. Businesses were trashed and left in rubble, while peaceful protesters fled the scene to safety. Masked looters were caught on camera, with images showing up on Twitter, Facebook and Instagram. Policemen were called to the scene. Some were harassed, and others did the harassing. Policemen began using what they call 'sound cannons', and the fire from these cannons caused a concentrated, painful sound wave over a long distance, to achieve crowd control. Within an hour, social media began attacking both the policemen and the rioters. Uninvolved civilians from around the globe began chiming in with their input. Ferguson was suddenly thrust to the center of the world.

By this time, I knew that whatever we were planning for our joint firm presentation on the research in North County had to be scrapped. I saw people whom I had interviewed earlier in the week--people whom I had surveyed on their opinions of the county. Now, they were taking to the streets with bullhorns, and their voices were being heard more clearly than I could have ever presented with data. They were upset with their local government. A tragedy had occurred, and St. Louis was now perceived as a national abomination — from the outside, Ferguson is St. Louis.

On Monday, August 11, I sent this e-mail to Aaron Perlut of Elasticity, and Katy Jamboretz, the Contractor Administrator for the Partnership:

> *Just curious if you guys think we need to process on the 2nd phase at this time or just wrap up the first one and give this unfortunate and horrible tragedy sometime to fade. I just can't*

see anything positive resonating for a while. Tensions are very high and this is becoming another Trayvon like situation unfortunately.

My own frustration and anger over Michael Brown's death contributed to my cynicism that Ferguson could ever be mended. And over the next few days, I watched as it got worse.

Later that day, there was a protest outside of the Ferguson Police Department. Death threats were made to the police department, and several civilians were arrested for unruly behavior. Police Chief Tom Jackson, who had planned to release the name of the shooting officer, retracted his plan over safety concerns. Later that night, protests once again turned into riots. Police forces claimed not to have military-grade weapons and armor, but were seen at night in riot gear, throwing cans of tear gas at protesters, peaceful and non-peaceful alike, in an attempt to quickly disperse the gathered crowd. Police dogs were deployed for crowd control, harkening back to the days of the civil rights movement. Media outlets around the country began running stories depicting Ferguson's authorities as incompetent and destructive. Ferguson itself came to be portrayed as a lawless wasteland.

On Tuesday, August 12, I immersed myself in the community with other members of my team from the Devin James Group. We went to various protest locations, along with pastors and other community leaders, touring the war zone that had been created. Our goal was to gather testimony from the disengaged residents and protestors, and find out what they thought the largest challenges in the community were. I wanted to present these findings to the Partnership in hopes that they would see what the black community was enduring. I wanted to make it clear to these predominantly white firms that this unrest stemmed from real emotions from real people, and that this matter would not be fixed by kicking off some public relations campaign to change perceptions and distract people into thinking that things are better.

The black community of Ferguson made one thing very clear to my team and me: things in Ferguson were a lot worse than the public understood. They thought that the leaders were not listening to them, and thus, were not representing them the way that true leaders should.

During the day of August 12, I received a response to the letter that I had sent the members of the partnership. Aaron Perlut wrote to both Katy and me:

> These events obviously make challenges on phase 1 and 2 far more difficult, but they also present us with an opportunity, a low point and thus a platform to build off of. It gives us a galvanizing moment where we can call for unity in North County. It would require us to find two people, one white and one black, non-governmental, who could work together to help rebuild the fabric of the North County community.

I remember reading that e-mail, and feeling my heart sink to the bottom of my stomach. My world stopped for a split second. I couldn't talk; I couldn't think. It felt like my gut was being wrung out like a wet towel. I couldn't believe it.

Could Aaron really feel like Michael Brown's death was a platform? Was this a real business e-mail, or was I just daydreaming? There was no way, in my mind, that someone claiming to have so much experience in PR, would be that enthusiastic about spinning this into a PR campaign. Was he really being insensitive? I thought. Or just ignorant? (Or both?). This actually would be the perfect opportunity for a real conversation to have taken place.

I felt disturbed by the revelation that my friend might be one of "those people" who says things like "those people," and uses the media for his own gain in the middle of a cultural crisis. I didn't want to believe it, but the only alternative was that he simply did not see Michael Brown's death as its own tragedy. It was simple to see that nothing positive would come out of the implementation of a high-level public relations campaign.

I took a few minutes to think it over, but I was still angry. I typed up a heated e-mail, but remembering my tweet a few days earlier, I didn't send it. I spent about 30 minutes re-drafting a new e-mail so that I didn't go completely off on this guy. Even as a communications expert, I struggled to find the "politically correct" words to use, but I knew that this was different. In this case, showing my true emotions would be counterproductive. Instead, I drafted up a long-winded e-mail. It read:

Katie and Aaron, this is great in theory but much more complicated because local police and government has already responded to this poorly and aggressively which created an even greater divide between communities in the county and people, and between people and the government.

To be honest, the research is now obsolete, because if we went back and asked everyone now what they thought of North County as a benchmark, you would see even more negative responses and diminished perceptions. Emotions and tensions created by this tragedy have changed the country's perception of North County and the City of St. Louis. As I said before, this is possibly worse than the Trayvon Martin shooting, and tanks and tear gas on the streets don't make for a good time to be talking about a branding initiative when there is a greater civil and human rights violation before us . . .

We can market and pr until we're blue in the face, but it won't move the needle of the public perception . . . this "galvanizing moment" is going to have to come internally, but even then, it won't happen until policemen are trialed and people have time to heal. I was on the ground last night as media was asked to leave as residents were threatening to get their machine guns and fight back by taking police officers' lives.

I think what Aaron and sometimes government entities forget is that these people rioting and looting are people. They are angry and displacing their anger. They may have different views on ways of conducting themselves, but they are people, and they feel the county has neglected them for so long, and they are not viewed as important. So something substantial has to be done on multiple levels or else we need to do nothing at all until the smoke clears.

Much in the same way that I explained earlier in this book, I took the time to respond to Aaron's email in a thoughtful, critical, yet inviting way, speaking my truth. My moral compass was right on. I was asking a question. I had a conscience and that physical feeling I had was cognitive dissonance and, for sure, when Aaron read what I wrote he was feeling the same thing and instantly went to a victim role (safety mode) not to have the conversation because in his mind, he was not a racist. But it was not about him at that moment. It was about not having a clear idea (or a good idea for that matter). Aaron was well off the mark, and I called him on it, but his lapse was due to a lack of cultural competence (a concept I will address later), a problem shared by many of us. Not a single one of us has all the knowledge so we build it together like the president and his cabinet. Democracy right? If you are a team then you rely on your teammates to keep you sharp and on your game.

As iron sharpens iron, so one person sharpens another.

(Proverbs 27:17).

This does not happen if folks are not honest and humble.

I felt that my background offered a much different perspective to those in power. Perspective can be a game-changer in the work force, which is why it is crucial to employ a diverse body of people—not just sex and gender, or race and ethnicity, but social, educational and financial diversity as well. That is truly the only way you can have a culturally sensitive and competent workplace. Having a room full of different life experiences enhances all areas of your potential because it continues to challenge your perspective, especially when dealing in spaces concerning equity, unless their concern really is not equity or they just don't know how to do something that requires courage and conscience.

When I said that Aaron had a lapse in judgment, I didn't mean it as an attack. It was an observation that my brothers and I had made over the years as black men in the business industry: a cultural incompetence. I have cultural incompetence, too, and I will never see the world through the same lens as a white, Asian, or Latino person. But in this situation he was in a position of power and had access to the information I had; he should have known better.

A few minutes later, Aaron responded in e-mail to only me:

Let me just wipe the bus tracks off my shirt...

This phrase and this behavior (victim) is a part of cognitive dissonance and it's a safety mechanism. Yes—dissonance (like when you hear music and it doesn't sound right [out of harmony], so you have a physical reaction to it). What you believe, what you know, what you do has to line up, and often times when trying to make a living you may be asked to do something or make a decision based upon principles.

> *The emotions of man are stirred more quickly than man's intelligence; and, as I pointed out some time ago in an article on the function of criticism, it is much more easy to have sympathy with suffering than it is to have sympathy with thought.*
>
> *-Oscar Wilde*

A few minutes later, he responded to everyone, following a phone call in which I was not included. Here, he addressed me while copying Katy and Mark Sutherland, his second-in-command at Elasticity. He wrote:

> *Thanks for your perspective, Devin. I'm not sure my thoughts were particularly well articulated, so I'll just wait until we all reconnect in person or on the phone, since this is clearly a sensitive and highly volatile issue.*

I do not believe Aaron was intentionally insensitive at all. On the surface, it's great that he's addressing it as a "sensitive and highly volatile issue." I would agree. But it's safe to say that he didn't feel that way in the first e-mail he sent, since he only addressed it after my response. In his first e-mail, all we had to do was round up one black guy, one white guy, and we'd all hold hands and sing Kumbaya. And if I had been like most of the other black folks in power in St. Louis, that is exactly what we would have done. That's not my style. Simply put, I didn't think the idea was smart. I thought that it was culturally insensitive and utterly ridiculous, and I wish I could have said what I was really thinking. Somehow, for standing up against the cultural atrocities being shoved in my face, I offended Aaron. He made it personal and about him, while not thinking about how what he was suggesting would affect 1) the team; 2) the work the team was about to do; 3) people in the black community in Ferguson; 4) the black community in the entire US.

> *It's in the act of having to do things that you don't want to that you learn something about moving past the self. Past the ego.*
>
> *-bell hooks*

Everyone else felt that I had thrown Aaron under the bus as well. And that makes sense because all of them were white and had similar backgrounds. That experience was the first instance in which I felt cornered, and helpless to do anything to change it. Soon, I would learn that this level of exclusion would rise like a wave and wash over the entire African-American community.

> *I contend that the cry of "black power" is, at bottom, a reaction to the reluctance of white power to make the kind of changes necessary to make justice a reality for the Negro. I think that we've got to see that a riot is the language of the unheard.*
> *-Martin Luther King Jr.*

On Wednesday, August 13, four days after the shooting, Ferguson policemen collectively decided to remove their nametags. They claim that it was for unity, but I think that it was likely for self-preservation purposes. In the evening, policemen were caught on camera allegedly violating the rights of journalists. In two separate instances, police arrested reporters and confiscated their cameras at a McDonald's near the scene of the shooting. President Obama, among others, called it a clear violation of the First Amendment. In another bout of rioting, an innocent camera crew from Al Jazeera America was hit with a can of tear gas. The scene was filmed by a bystander, and showed the crew fleeing from the tear gas. Moments later, the law enforcement officials tended to the camera equipment, turning it all off and removing it from the scene. Nearby, St. Louis officials were arrested with several others for allegedly not listening to law enforcement commands.

CHAPTER 4

CODENAME NORTH COUNTY: IDENTIFYING THE CRISIS

ON AUGUST 14TH, the Partnership called for an impromptu meeting at their headquarters in Clayton, Missouri, the heart of St. Louis County. It was the first time I would visit their headquarters after Michael Brown's death.

The meeting was meant for the members to convene and focus on the state of emergency within North County. All of the key players in the area were slated to attend. I still had yet to meet any of the members of Common Ground PR, but from my years in St. Louis, I knew that they were hailed as the best in the area. I was looking forward to seeing what they had to say.

REMOVING MICHAEL BROWN

We arrived at the building in the early morning. At approximately 11:40 a.m., we watched President Obama address the nation. He talked about the Department of Justice's intent to investigate the death of Michael Brown, and called for both peaceful protesting by the people and peaceful allowance of protest by the police forces. He mentioned the journalists who had been arrested simply for doing their job. It was helpful to have federal acknowledgement of the injustices committed within Ferguson borders, despite the political talking points that Obama made during his speech.

Leaders from the churches, local politicians, and the Partnership itself were present at the meeting. The Chief Executive Officers for some of the largest companies in the region were conferenced in through telephone. Both my firm and Elasticity were introduced to everyone in attendance.

Before long, we were all asked to take a seat. All I could think of was the fact that I hadn't been introduced to anyone from Common Ground. I turned to Aaron as I eased back into my chair. I didn't feel much like talking to him at the moment, but my curiosity had gotten the better of me.

"Where the hell is Common Ground?" I asked.

"They're not here. They're in Ferguson working on a PR strategy."

"Damn," I said. "Then how are they supposed to get anything out of this?"

Aaron just shrugged his shoulders, as though he had never really given it any thought.

Denny Coleman, a power player at the Partnership, stood up at the head of the table. A wrinkle in his forehead showed a burly exhaustion, and his hands gripped the arm of his leather chair like a stress ball. He looked like he was ready to blow at any minute.

Denny thanked the audience for meeting under what was proving to be a colossal nightmare for St. Louis County and the surrounding region. He stated that he was there to announce a change of direction moving forward.

Denny told us that the Partnership would be focusing more of its efforts to help Ferguson. He stated that it was clear that the city needed help controlling the PR and marketing fiasco that could stand to cost the region billions of dollars. He stressed that Ferguson's failure inherently meant the failure of St. Louis County and the state of Missouri itself.

I agreed with Denny in that St. Louis's future legacy rested on the work that we were to conduct in the coming months in Ferguson, but I disagreed with him on two key points. First, I didn't think we could "save Ferguson." Ferguson had changed. The idea of saving Ferguson originates from that white savior complex; the legacy he wanted to maintain was that of white supremacy.

At this point the damage had been done. It needed to be acknowledged, and an apology needed to be given to the black community for all the abuse and mistreatment it had endured over the years. We simply needed to move forward in order to create a new Ferguson. There was no spare tire for this one. I felt that we needed to change the entire car, and then put it on a different street, headed in a completely different direction. We needed to head towards upward mobility, an unbiased court system, quality healthcare, financial literacy, and equity-focused community policing and building. If Ferguson were to ever again be seen as a healthy thriving community, we would need to first admit that there was a longstanding racial tension in the community that had only recently come to light--tension that existed back to and before the days of Senator Rita Days' migration to St. Louis.

> *I began to use the phrase in my work white supremacist capitalist patriarchy because I wanted to have some language that would actually remind us continually of the interlocking systems of domination that define our reality and not to just have one thing be like, you know, gender is the important issue, race is the important issue, but for me the use of that particular jargonistic phrase was a way, a sort of short cut way of saying all of these things actually are functioning simultaneously at all times in our lives and that if I really want to understand what's happening to me, right now at this moment in my life, as a black female of a certain age group, I won't be able to understand it if I'm only looking through the lens of race. I won't be able to understand it if I'm only looking through the lens of gender. I won't be able to understand it if I'm only looking at how white people see me.*

> *To me an important breakthrough, I felt, in my work and that of others was the call to use the term white supremacy, over racism because racism in and of itself did not really allow for a discourse of colonization and decolonization, the recognition of the internalized racism within people of color and it was always in a sense keeping things at the level at which whiteness and white people remained at the center of the discussion. In my classroom I might say to students that you know that when we use the term white supremacy it doesn't just evoke white people, it evokes a political world that we can all frame ourselves in relationship to....*

> *And so for me those words were very much about the constant reminder, one of institutional construct, that we're not talking about personal construct in the sense of, how do you feel about me as a woman, or how do you feel about me as a black person?*

-- *bell hooks*

Personally, I thought that people should have been the focus of the planning, and not monetary profits or losses. Coleman made it sound like the main focus should be on the county and state's reputations, then the big businesses in the region. I couldn't understand why his focus wasn't on community engagement—making things better for the people, specifically the black community, and any disenfranchised and underserved communities. I thought that the meeting should have begun acknowledging their pain.

After Denny finished his briefing, he took a seat and turned the presentation over to Katy, the Partnership's Communications Team Leader. She stated that the Partnership had been working with Ferguson officials in the few days following the tragedy, and it was clear that there was a lot going on that would severely damage the region if it ever reached the media.

Interesting, I thought, so what does she know that we don't?

I can't say that I was too surprised at what she was divulging. In crisis management mode, many government entities go into lockdown, instead of finding a way to disclose their mistakes to the public in a culturally relevant and meaningful way. Then follow with lies, cover-ups, and excuses. In government, it's an all-too-common business practice.

She went on to disclose that Ferguson had already received numerous Freedom of Information Act (FOIA), or "Sunshine" requests. She stated that everyone, from media reporters to FOIA terrorists, was bombarding the City Clerk and Attorney with FOIA requests. She advised us that we had to act swiftly if we were going to defend our region.

I thought, Swiftly? Defend? What did we have to defend against?

I wouldn't find that out until later.

Katy continued, stating that the single greatest thing that we had working in our favor was Ferguson's small population. She explained that for larger cities, the law provides that sunshine requests must be met and returned in full within days, or even hours. In a city the size of Ferguson, where most of the working officials are only part-time or volunteering, it is much less reasonable to return any sunshine request in that short of a time period. She stated that this single fact could be our saving grace, but that the Partnership's communications team was prepared for even that to fall through. She eventually told us that the Partnership would be implementing a keyword restriction initiative. The Partnership's new rule prohibited anyone working for the Partnership from using those key words in any of their texts, e-mails, or any other thread of documented communication. This is because in the few days following Michael Brown's death, nearly every sunshine request submitted to Ferguson contained either or both of the terms "Ferguson" and "Michael Brown."

Listening to her speech, I shook my head the same way I did with Aaron's e-mail. *They are clueless,* I thought. Clueless and egotistical about real people and what happens to them because that's not their main concern.

In most government work, almost everything we do is documented or recorded, not only for public records, but also for our own protection. Meetings are typically recorded in order to transcribe information for absent team members, and to define a clear path for the next steps following the meeting, including tasks and deliverables. When a meeting is not recorded or documented, it is because someone doesn't want it to be. This is a simple truth known throughout the public sector. The Partnership's new initiative was not only questionable, but highly unethical, and further proved that the Partnership was not working to address the systemic racial issues or to benefit the people impacted. If they were, they would have had no reason to try to evade having their documents found. It was a sleazy approach, but typical. The only thing that bothered me more was that the people sitting around me, even the black leaders, were all nodding their heads in agreement. Maybe they were all in on it, since the initiative would only further protect their positions, investments, and preserve their reputations. With an initiative like that in place, how could they not have already been planning on it?

If I were really doing the work they asked me to do for "community engagement," then I would be interrupting the status quo. People in government are so fearful of this because my work could lead to their having to deal with the real issues. Themselves.

We have to embrace new models of dealing with our issues in this country if we are to truly change as a nation.

WORKING FROM A DISTANCE

The Partnership began scrambling to get their PR firms to announce things like new jobs, job fairs, and facility expansions. They dispatched the Urban League and other capacity building organizations to attempt to suppress tensions within the black community. The Partnership even announced a "recovery fund" that was supposed to help small businesses. Then, the Partnership sent Common Ground (in conjunction with Elasticity) in to reduce the perception of the threat and losses to the region.

I am not saying that the Partnership shouldn't have been worried about the economy. However, not one conversation was about people, or more specifically, black people. There was no talk of the root of the unrest in Ferguson. This was an immediate alert to me that things were not slated to go well.

The leaders of the Partnership submitted to the corporations' wishes as though they were being held at gunpoint. None of the other firms had any interest in truly helping the people. Few, if any, representatives from any global corporation housed in St. Louis County had even set foot in Ferguson since the shooting. There were representatives from Emerson and Express Scripts who were only present when we held the "high-level" meetings at Florissant Valley Community College, and when the Governor or media were present. Additionally, these meetings were always orchestrated so that community members were never in attendance. The corporate representatives who did attend stayed clear of the "problem areas" like ground zero (the site of the Quicktrip burned down by the Ferguson riots) and most of West Florissant. They knew very little about the protests in the community, or the people engaged in social warfare on the outside of those walls (except the times when they'd happen to catch a news clip, portraying a violent, angry crowd.) All of the meetings were set up for the public to listen to the officials speak. The officials never wanted feedback from any of the members of the black community, who were protesting in order to obtain a platform to speak and have an equal voice.

The people who truly understood what was going on were the protesters, the ones out there getting their hands dirty and rolling up their sleeves. I previously mentioned going into the crowd of protestors with community and religious leaders at my side. I did not mention the heat from the Molotov's I felt as they landed nearby, engulfing a family-owned business in a set of flames. I did not mention getting spit on, and I did not mention the bottles of urine thrown at the police that often hit myself or my crew after being redirected several times by the crowd.

As I proceeded to interact with the Ferguson officials and corporate representatives, I realized that this group had no idea what the issues were. None of their suggestions were appropriate. The unrest in the region obviously had been simmering for decades, and the officials only wanted to make it appear normal to the people and investors outside the region. The officials wanted to present this information like it wasn't indicative of how business was conducted in Missouri.

All I could think was, this is exactly how they do business in Missouri.

OUR NEW ASSIGNMENT

Because we were the only minority firm working with the Partnership at the time, we were assigned the task of developing a community outreach and engagement strategy for Ferguson. We were instructed to focus specifically on Ferguson, instead of North County at large. This meant that we would be traveling to Ferguson City Hall to meet with the city's administrators daily. But before all of that happened, we needed to have a plan in place, and we had to prepare for a crisis from every angle.

I thought this would be a perfect time for me to take my own advice about crisis forecasting and revisit my criminal background and past before I moved forward. I knew that I had disclosed it in writing prior to my firm being contracted, but I wanted to disclose it again for clarification. For anyone to suggest that I made it to this table, advising an elite group of individuals, without disclosing my past, is foolish. Anyone who contracts with the government knows that this is the highest level of scrutiny one can face, and very common for the government to check one's background, credit and drug history prior to contracting. Even if you apply for a job at McDonald's, you have to get a background check! Aaron Perlut from Elasticity, County Executive Charlie Dooley, Denny Coleman and Katy Jamboretz from the Partnership were all aware of my past. In fact, it was one of the reasons that she thought I would be a great fit for North County in the first place.

While working in both the national and international media spotlight, we were reminded that every time we made a move, the world was watching.

I asked, "Why do we change what we would do because the world is watching?"

CHAPTER 5

THE BELLY
OF THE BEAST

I LEFT THE MEETING at the Partnership's office with a sour taste in my mouth. My team was instructed to go to Ferguson City Hall and meet up with the leadership team from Common Ground PR, who had already been working in Ferguson since the day of the shooting. We were slated to learn what they had planned for the city moving forward.

It was a general consensus that the Devin James Group would be the firm to get in on the ground floor in Ferguson. We were thankful for this opportunity, because my own background and the diversity of my firm gave us a more unique perspective--one that the rest of the firms and the

Partnership severely lacked. More importantly, I knew what kind of man I was. I am someone with roots in an underserved community, with a burning desire to help the disadvantaged reach new levels of productivity. My roots and life experiences enable me to see situations from a perspective of equity, and not a perspective that assumes everyone has the same levels of resources and support. I do not have the ability to see abuse and to look the other way. I care about more than money. I believe in community.

THE NATTA ROOM

Ferguson may have had the national spotlight at the time, but it is still a small town with a very humble infrastructure. City Hall, a faded brick building, is located at 110 Church Street. If you were only casually passing by, you might miss it. The building was nestled in between two slightly taller buildings on the patchy two-lane street.

We met in the Natta Room. Instead of thick, plush leather chairs like at the Partnership's office, there was an old-school vibe that let you know nothing had been updated or remodeled in at least 20 years. Chairs rocked when you sat in them, and the large conference table looked worn. The room had a burgundy and green design style to reflect Ferguson's logo, and it gave off a largely outdated feel.

I sat next to Peggy Killian, who served as the copywriter for Common Ground PR. Next to her was Denise Bentele, Common Ground's lead publicist and CEO. I recognized her from photographs I had seen in several online publications. It was the first time that I had met anyone from Common

Ground, and the first impression was slightly weird. They were dressed like soccer moms compared to their usual glammed out presentation from the photos and articles I had seen, so I was taken aback. They noticed my confusion and they quickly pointed out that this was their "incognito" look for Ferguson.

"Devin James," I said, and offered my hand.

"Thanks for joining us, Devin," Denise beamed. They both seemed very well put together, and incredibly calm, like they were prepared for battle. When I shook both of their hands, though, they felt a little preoccupied, like their minds were on something else.

"I've been looking forward to working side by side," she said. She wanted to let us know that she respected the presence of our firm.

Denise continued, "I can't wait to see what your firm has planned for us."

"Planned?" I thought. "Aren't we all here to learn your plan?"

The other people in the room didn't have the same level of poise as than Common Ground. Ferguson's City Clerk Megan Askainen, City Manager John Shaw, and City Attorney Stephanie Karr were also present. Keep in mind here that, although these people were all professionals, they had just been accused of being part of one of the most racially charged officer-involved shootings of the year, and this office was the eye of the storm. I can't say I blamed them for being a little bit nervous.

When I stepped back and took in the entire room, I noticed that my firm and I were the only minorities.

I couldn't help thinking, as I saw Megan chewing at her fingernails, and John with his eyes focused on nothing in particular, "What can privileged white people who can't even see that there is a racial divide possibly implement to resolve a hurt and angry community of African Americans?"

Denise stood up and walked to the edge of the room, where there was a small whiteboard littered with talking points they had compiled from previous meetings.

Megan addressed the group: "Thank you all for meeting with us today. I'd like to introduce you all to Mr. Devin James and his firm, the Devin James Group. They will be assisting us in creating a community engagement plan."

I soon learned that the reason I was called in was because the city and the partnership (specifically their PR team Common Ground) did not have a plan on how to engage the black community of Ferguson to begin with. With no more than a few talking points on the whiteboard, Common Ground PR was completely stuck on where to go next. Denise and Peggy were hoping that my firm could swoop in and tell them all that needed to be done.

Where did that leave me? On one hand, I was flattered that one of the best PR firms in the city needed me to perform community engagement work. In the PR industry, Denise and Aaron are like my elders. They've been working longer and come from big agencies. Most would consider it an honor to work with them. Although I did consider it an honor to work with them, I also realized that they were only trying to protect themselves in the media and save face with industry peers.

THE HUMBLING

Months later, the Department of Justice announced that it would reveal its plan to investigate Ferguson for civil rights violations. The findings report, which came out only a few weeks after the announcement of the investigation, revealed the same chilling details that my firm found during our early days in the Natta Room.

No one who was a participant in the scandal considered themselves a racist in the slightest bit. Most were offended whenever I brought up the tough topics we needed to address concerning race. And many of the others just didn't have their eyes and ears open, or the moral compass to see what they were contributing to.

> White fragility is, at its essence, gut level pushback. It's like the fight or flight response of white people who want to believe that they, and the world by extension, are less racially divisive than they really are. It's when you feel like the wind has been knocked out of you when a person of color points out that something you've said seems rooted in a privileged experience of the world. It's when you desperately want to defend why a well-intentioned institution that you're a part of isn't really racist.
>
> -Robin DiAngelo

The people making decisions every day were just employees to the machine. The racist system set up hundreds of years ago is now law, and working people enforce the system without questioning its structure. They are just coming to work, getting a check, and providing for their families. Many of them don't see the system for what it is, because the system helps them to survive.

Systemic racism starts with the people who started and manage the system. Ferguson's system was flawed far before the days of Dred Scott. The system is indoctrinated into our everyday consciousness—in order to change or even address the system, one must change society's policies. Protesting can bring attention to the issues, but one needs to change tangible documents (the policies and the laws), and then address the behaviors by incorporating accountability. Many city employees were only pushing the buttons and pulling the levers. Any of them could be replaced, and the same results would occur. Replacing the people without changing the policies does nothing but perpetuate previous attitudes and behaviors. After all, many people have been desensitized to the abuse and mistreatment of black people. This can be remedied by introducing concepts with an equitable lens for people to see perspectives different from their own.

I stayed in Ferguson because I wanted to make sure that among the understandably panicked city officials, there was someone who was working for the interest of the black community. People developed scathing attitudes toward me because I was not from Ferguson or St. Louis. I never viewed that as a bad thing because to me, racial issues weren't geographically specific.

CHAPTER 6

THE CHARACTER ASSASSINATION

ON AUGUST 14, I was introduced to both the Police Chief and the Mayor of Ferguson. I was pretty skeptical about both of them. It wasn't because they were white or because I thought they were racists, but because of the chilling precedent that had been set by their staff and their contractors that same day.

Of course, I had my own issues with the Chief himself. "Tom Jackson," the stout Chief of Police said to me. He offered his large hand. To him, it was a simple handshake, but to me, it was a much greater story.

"Devin James," I said. I shook his hand, firmly like I was always raised to. I made eye contact, directly. But I didn't smile. I couldn't bring myself to. Here was a man who symbolized everything that I had been raised to fear.

I knew that I had never met this man before. I had no reason to fear or hate the man. But this is at a time when anyone who's black and raising a son is terrified. Chief Jackson, among the other Ferguson officials, had been given a comprehensive briefing of my firm from the Partnership, which included details about my criminal background. When I looked into the Chief's eyes, I saw myself in the reflection. I saw myself as a young boy, stealing from local stores to feed my family. I saw myself a little older, being stopped for jaywalking, and wondering if I would make it home that evening. I saw myself being handcuffed while I was just standing at a gas station selling some of my music to people who pulled up. I saw my possessions being stripped from my car when they illegally searched it and pinned me to the ground. I saw Sergeant Mullins, from the Memphis Police Department, whose investigation resulted in my felony conviction. I saw criminal court Judge Chris Craft, and all the belittling comments he made, and my mind went back to that smirk on his face when he sentenced me to prison.

I felt bad for having these feelings toward someone to whom I had never spoken more than my name. But any black man or woman would tell you that they feel the same way anytime they step into the shadow of a law enforcement officer.

I broke the handshake (something I was taught never to do), I dismissed the thoughts, and turned to the mayor, James Knowles III.

I shook his hand.

I had studied Mayor Knowles before meeting him, so I knew a little bit about his background. I knew that he was chairman of Missouri's Young Republicans chapter. I knew that he was a go-getter politician, beating out an incumbent mayor in a city election in 2011, making him the youngest mayor in Ferguson's history at age 31. I also knew that voter turnout was very low in that election, especially among African-Americans.

From the outset, my only problem with the mayor was that I couldn't get a good read on him. It seemed that he and I were about the same age, so I figured I could relate to him a bit. But as I listened to him talk about the struggle of African-Americans in Ferguson, it sounded like he was reading out of a textbook rather than reciting from his own experiences. He mentioned "white privilege" a few too many times, and he slipped in the fact that he took a black girl to a dance in high school.

THE SENSITIVITY TEST

Given the nature of the crisis, we didn't have a lot of time to get to know the people inside Ferguson. I wasn't able to sit down for coffee with Mayor Knowles and assess his character or his cultural competency. All I had to go on was what I had heard from others, the media and what I had seen in my initial interactions with him and the Chief. But I still needed to know them inside and out in order to create a working plan moving forward. In other words, I needed to know where their hearts were.

I hired an experienced organizational psychologist to develop a customized race and cultural sensitivity test. The test consisted of various questions that were to be presented to the city officials in order to demonstrate things like racial or gender bias, cultural competence and sensitivity, as well as to help with understanding views and stereotypes. We also included some uneven resources exercises.

The test looked great, but there was one problem. I knew that if I were to administer the test on paper, they would not only be skeptical, but they would do their best to fudge the data and try to pass, instead of showing their true selves. So instead of printing it out, my team and I devised a strategy to administer it orally by casually working the questions into conversation over the course of a couple of days. Some we even weaved into interview prep questions.

To my surprise, the Chief passed with flying colors! I figured from the moment I met him that he would be the most problematic, but that was my own bias speaking. I still didn't know whether or not he was truly a racially ethical person, but at least he had some form of cultural training, and that was working in his favor.

The mayor, on the other hand, did the worst out of anyone. He was inappropriate in his demeanor, and he casually threw out insensitive comments. The biggest problem was that none of the insensitivity was intentional. Passive racism was embedded in him, and I didn't have any indication that he was attempting to turn it around. There was no accountability within the city. No one corrected him. Part of it may be because he is a large man. Standing at 6'5 and being nearly 260 pounds, I'm sure that he intimidates some people. But he also has a confrontational demeanor. He never backs down from the opportunity to debate, even when he's wrong. He is a natural politician. It didn't help that there were barely any minorities on the staff to set him straight.

A Great Plan Gone Wrong

On the afternoon of August 14, we sat around the table in the Natta Room once again. Peggy and Denise from Common Ground sat to my left. City Manager John Shaw, City Clerk Megan Asikainen, City Attorney Stephanie Karr, Chief Tom Jackson, Assistant Chief Al Eickhoff, and Mayor Knowles sat across the table. My team sat to my right.

Although the mayor was the symbolic leader of the city, John Shaw actually ran the gears of the operation. At the advice of Common Ground, John had been encouraging the mayor to make media appearances to keep people's focus off of himself. I immediately advised that was a stupid idea. I told them the only reason the Mayor should be on camera was if he was delivering a public apology.

But on this day, we were discussing the release of the name of the officer who killed Mike Brown.

"This has been a long-awaited announcement," John said, "We were supposed to make it a few days ago, but decided against it for the sake of safety. But now, the media is attacking us from all angles, and they won't be satisfied until we release the officer's name."

Good, I thought, but this shouldn't be about making the media happy. This should be about the Brown family and the Black community. They have the right to know. Stephanie interrupted,

"In regards to the FOIA request, we are obligated to go through with this to give people the whole story."

"What do you mean?" I said.

Stephanie said, "Mike Brown was involved in a robbery minutes before the shooting. We have video footage of the incident, and the media believes that it's the public's right to know. We are planning to release this video in conjunction with the officer's name."

I stopped her in mid-speech. "No," I said. "If Michael Brown robbed a store, that's for someone else to look into. The robbery had nothing to do with the shooting. The Chief himself said that the officer wasn't aware of the robbery when he shot him."

I looked to the Chief for confirmation, I could tell he didn't agree with them but he didn't say anything. It looked like they had already made their minds up and he had to just follow orders.

"Devin," Stephanie said, "this isn't about context. It's about compliance and the release of information that the people have the right to know."

"That's understandable, but very insensitive," I said. "It's the wrong move. Maybe the people have a right to know, but releasing the video at the same time as you release the name is fucking ridiculous. You have no idea what you're doing."

I looked around the room. Everyone seemed to be on board with this. Maybe they just didn't care. They didn't seem to understand that in the eyes of the black community, they had already killed Brown, and then disrespected his remains by leaving his body in the street for so long. Now, they were about to kill his character.

"Don't do this," I said. "You need to eat this one. If you do this, you may not be able to bounce back. The black community will never forgive you. In their eyes, you *all* killed and disrespected Michael Brown. Don't kill and disrespect him again."

No matter how much I pled, they would not listen.

I later found out that the Department of Justice had also previously approached the City of Ferguson regarding the robbery video, but the language used to describe their approach in their reports was much stronger and more specific than the communications that actually took place. Representatives from the DOJ told the city that they would issue a document that would prohibit the release of the video for safety. But after repeated request, they never furnished the document and St. Louis County Police, the FBI and others were all encouraging the city and Chief to release the video. Contrary to reports or articles, there was no long discussion from the DOJ to the city about why they shouldn't release the video. The DOJ could have prevented a lot of the chaos and damage that resulted from the video being released if they had just honored their word about the document to stop it. Instead they went unresponsive, which meant the Chief was going to take the blame for this horrible decision even though he was only the messenger.

Whenever you are facing something with this kind of capacity for a violent eruption, you need to frame the information with the right context. Ferguson Officials lacked the cultural sensitivity to understand why they shouldn't have released the video.

The experience proved that none of the professionals working in Ferguson had ever seen a real crisis. They surely didn't know what to do in a racial crisis between whites and African-American, or how to move Ferguson from reactive to proactive attitudes. I understood the real problem. One can't expect people to get over hundreds of years of abuse because of a hashtag or a campaign. The way I saw it, the old Ferguson was long gone. I was there to help rebuild a new one.

AGAINST MY BETTER JUDGMENT

In an attempt to loosen tensions in the black community, Ron Johnson, an African-American State Highway Patrol Captain, was appointed by the governor to oversee relations between protesters and the police department and manage security operations in the city of Ferguson. It was the Governor's hope that Johnson would be the leader that the African American community could get behind. Johnson encouraged the protestors to keep matters peaceful. At night, he was seen standing among the protesters, and even hugging them. For the first night since the tragedy, the city was relatively calm.

Unfortunately, that didn't last long. The next day, August 15, the Chief followed his orders and gave a live statement, which aired nationwide. He revealed that the officer in question was Darren Wilson, a 28-year-old policeman. He then announced the release of the robbery video, as well as accompanying records naming Michael Brown as the suspect.

Just as I had predicted, the video gave Darren Wilson supporters the fuel they needed to paint Brown as a bad person, and it gave Michael Brown supporters fuel to become even angrier with Ferguson government.

The video spread across social media. The same people who picketed in support of the police shared still frames from the video, with captions painting Brown as a criminal.

A bit later, Michael Brown's family publicly condemned the decision to release the video, calling it a direct attempt to assassinate their son's character.

They were right. Whether Brown was guilty of theft or not, the video was 100% irrelevant to the tragedy at hand. It was a very basic distraction. The Chief publicly admitted that Wilson had not known of the robbery at the time of the shooting. To me, it was painfully obvious that the video was released in an attempt to assassinate Brown's character.

It was a cheap move that the black community felt in its heart. We knew that theft had nothing to do with the shooting. The release of the video served as a complete manipulation of the public's perception of Brown, and was used as a pitiful defense to cover the police force and further justify Wilson's actions. By releasing the video, the media sent the message that Brown deserved to be shot. The historical context of this decision is important because it clearly serves as an example of demonizing black men. Disparities between blacks and whites are relevant in many aspects of American society, ranging from prison sentencing to entertainment. In recent years, prison sentences for black men are 20 percent longer than for white men who committed similar crimes.[10] This institutional bias even trickles down to sports and entertainment—when Tiger Woods' infidelity was revealed, he was dropped from many of his sponsors, and was battered and beaten by the media. When Brett Favre had the same thing happen, people laughed it off and forgave him.

The public levies harsher judgments on black people, and this is evident in many sectors of our society. I understood this aspect of race relations as I observed them make this decision.

Many think the Chief made the decision to release the robbery video but he didn't. In my personal conversations with him, he revealed to me that he never wanted to do it. I

[10] Pazallolo, Joe. "Racial Gap in Men's Sentencing." The Wall Street Journal. 14 Feb 2013. Web. Day May 2015.
http://www.wsj.com/articles/SB10001424127887324432004578304463789858002

believe him. He let them pressure him into doing it, and for that he is responsible. But the decision came directly from the city attorney.

That night, in anticipation that relations could turn violent, nearly all Ferguson businesses closed early and locked up their buildings to the best of their ability. Within hours, trucks circled with wood for business owners to board up their windows and glass. Shortly after nightfall, the protests turned violent. In an astonishingly short amount of time, both the police and National Guard brought their military vehicles and teams back into the streets. They began threatening the protesters with bullhorns and the use of tear gas, in an attempt to disperse the crowds. Officers took cover behind riot gear as they were pelted with rocks, urine-filled bottles, Molotov cocktails and pieces of trash.

The riots went on well into the night. While everyone behind the City Hall walls watched and waited, both my team and the Chief of Police worked through the night. In order to be prepared for the meetings and briefings in the mornings, we had to be working when all the action was taking place. We had to document, record, and synthesize each detail almost immediately because we had one continuous news cycle. We dealt with literal meltdowns from officers and city staff constantly. We served as community engagement strategists, head coaches, and therapists. The stress was very high, and very real. As an added problem, we never had a large chunk of time to train the officials because crises were happening around the clock.

Maybe the officials didn't realize that what they were doing was wrong. Maybe they knew, and they just didn't care to admit it. Either way, they were fueling the fire.

CHAPTER 7

COMMUNITY BARRIERS IDENTIFIED

ON AUGUST 16, Governor Jay Nixon swept into town and declared a curfew in Ferguson. Any protest, no matter how peaceful, suddenly became illegal during the late hours of the night. Although he intended to quell intentions in the community, Governor Nixon failed to recognize that making something illegal does not stop it from happening. Americans have made this fact clear for years, with its perpetual implementation of discriminatory practices against African-Americans across the country. Those who were assembling peacefully were now grouped in with those who were rioting and looting. Picture yourself in that position, as a peaceful protester who is yearning to be heard, but are instead told that you have to be inside by a certain time. Wouldn't that make you angry? It did for many people.

On the evening of August 17, my assistant and I left the Natta Room to head out into Ferguson. We started interviewing more protesters. We interviewed several community members who were standing by as well. Some protesters told us that they felt unheard and violated. According to them, it wasn't hard to see why Ferguson was in the national spotlight. They thought that the new curfew was an infringement on their rights, and I agreed with them wholeheartedly.

One of the main concerns was that nationally, the media painted Ferguson's protesters in a very negative light. Although there were people throwing Molotov's and shooting blindly into gathered crowds, there were several people protesting peacefully and standing in prayer circles singing hymns. We witnessed teenagers and children among the protestors, and the adults were educating them on how to peacefully assemble. The older protesters taught the children and teenagers the history of black protestors, and the urgency of being a careful black child while engaging in civil disobedience, because they were much more likely to be labeled as troublemakers and be assaulted.

Several national media outlets and activist groups hired many protestors to stage acts of disobedience in order to give their own sensationalist stories more bearing in the national spotlight. Many of the people on television and in Facebook and Twitter videos were actually civilians who were provoked or encouraged to act out for the sake of a good story. We had cameras, and people often thought that my crew was media. They would ask, "How much you gone pay us to act a fool?" We didn't mess with them. We only wanted to get into the eyes and the ears of the *real* hurt and pain in Ferguson: the Ferguson that was angry, fearful, and hopeless. We wanted to reach the people who lived there, who had to deal with the neglect, abuse and mistreatment every day. Only then could I turn my attention to the issues of the black community nationwide.

Still, it was hard for us to find a true leader of the protest. There were figureheads in the black community who were readily available to every media outlet every day but weren't actually doing anything for the black community in Ferguson.

One group maintained a tent directly across from the Ferguson Police station, sitting on the lot of Andy Wurm Tire and Wheel Company. One of the regular hosts of the tent was a brother named Orlando Brown. I met with Orlando one day after hours of protest at the police station. We had some mutual connections and life experiences, so we hit it off instantly. He was different from many of the others because he wasn't in it for money or any personal gain; like me, he was a black man and concerned father who overcame the odds.

His group expressed an interest in a meeting with the Chief and the City Manager, so I began coordinating meetings for his group to meet with the Chief first. The meetings were very informative for Ferguson officials, and together, they shared tips and ideas for organizing more peaceful protests to keep our people out of harm's way.

I believe this ultimately improved relations with some of the people who were once angry. Before meeting with him, if people in the tent saw me with either the Chief or Mayor, they would scream expletives and chant. After the meetings, I believe they got a chance to get to know me better, so I would often join his group at the tent for food and conversation where I would then advise them on the steps needed to move from chants to action. I would also talk about their concerns, talk about what the city and I were working on, and dispelled any rumors or issues that surfaced about my involvement. This is how I would demonstrate to the city officials and the police department what it meant to be "community conscious."

I addressed these concerns at the next few meetings with all key stakeholders, and I learned that every department had an established budget to "assist" with community engagement. But the money was allocated in a cryptic way, so nobody in the community (and specifically the black community) ever knew about it.

THE DIVISIVE WALL

In government, there is always a set of documents that set the rules and goals for the leaders. Countries have constitutions. Towns have charters. There are documents for strategic planning, economic development, community engagement, and more. There's always a document that you can look to and say, "This is our plan that includes the task to complete each deliverable. This is what we need to do to achieve our goal."

The same is true with religion, fraternities, sports, or any sort of official entity. But the African-American community in Ferguson did not have any such document, and no one was working on one, neither in government nor the community.

I looked at all the black leaders in St. Louis County government and I asked, "Where is your plan for our people?

What is the timeline to achieve our goal, and how can we accomplish it?"

It's foolish to think that anything in Ferguson could have
gotten done without a proper plan in place. The same is true
for the African-American community at large in this country.
Protests and demonstrations are important and necessary,
but they can only go so far and are really ineffective if they
are not part of a larger plan for the community. When I see
the black leaders who have the knowledge and charisma to
lead a real revolution, and I see them only looking to pad
their pockets, I see a growing wall between our community
and real systemic progress.

This was another night in which police forces used tear
gas on rallying protesters and media personnel. But the tear
gas, of course, did nothing to stop the emotions of the people
targeted. It only made things worse. In two instances, media
personnel were threatened by the police with more than just
words, including a reporter who was threatened with being
"shelled" by an officer if he kept his camera light on (the reporter complied, but was still met with backlash, and it's all
on video).

The next morning, Governor Nixon finally got the hint
from the previous few nights. He lifted the curfew and encouraged the community to engage in peaceful protest. As
the riots continued, more protesters were assaulted and harassed. The media displayed more and more videos of officers
acting both unconventionally and inhumanely. Some of
these videos were stretched attempts to paint officers in a
bad light. Others were disturbing reassurances of the continuing chaos.

On the night of Tuesday, August 19, a group of peaceful
protesters was interrupted when Officer Ray Albers of the St.

Ann Police Department had a cup of urine thrown his way. Several civilians with their cell phone cameras filmed Albers as he brandished a rifle and pointed it at the crowd. He yelled, "I will fucking kill you!" A man who was filming asked him for his name, and Albers replied, "Go fuck yourself!" He was quickly ushered away by another officer, who convinced him to put the gun down.

When the videos hit social media, Albers became a poster man for the unrest in Ferguson. He was both ridiculed and rebuked, while people safe at home on Facebook and Reddit began to call him "Officer Go Fuck Yourself." It was a new low for the image of the city and its representatives. What's worse is that, while all of the raucous stories made the front page, the stories of the children being taught their rights and their history were not found so easily. The media just wasn't into that. My firm was charged with handling media. We pitched positive story after positive story to various media outlets, but they only wanted to show four things: black people "acting a fool," government misconduct or scandal-related stories, people getting hurt by law enforcement and capturing property damage.

The riots continued, and though there were fewer incidents in the next days, the spotlight was still hot. On August 20, United States Attorney General Eric Holder arrived in Missouri, effectively putting the federal government's stamp on the Ferguson tragedy. The Department of Justice initiated its investigation on Ferguson, adding more stress to the underprepared administrators working in Ferguson City Hall.

My team and I continued to attend rallies and meet with those gathered in the community in an effort to stop the misrepresentation from happening on both sides. Back at the Natta Room, we drew up a document laying out their top concerns, which we called *Community Barriers Identified*. On August 20, we presented it to the rest of the Partnership and the City of Ferguson administration and officials. It read:

Team,

I am just getting in from protest and watching various news segments and had my team monitoring social media trending. As you know we have quite a few major things coming up (possible indictment or not, and Mike Brown Funeral) so I want us to begin dialogue about things we can do to get in front of issues and upcoming events instead of always coming from behind having to clean/clear up, be defensive and/or do damage control.

Some of this may appear basic but here are the barriers we have identified.

Community Barriers:

- **Stigmas, Rumors, Misinformed or uninformed and Misconceptions:** *Most of the media and the community don't have the facts straight and don't know who is responsible for what. Tons of people are assuming things and many people are being attacked from the Ferguson Mayor to Common Ground PR.*

- **Violent Protestor Behaviors:** *This continues to give the city troubles with perceptions particularly online, on social media and with traditional media.*

- **Politics and Personal Agendas:** *There are so many political figures jumping at every camera opportunity they can get: some officials are throwing others' under* *the bus, while others are simply appearing so off based that their lack of articulation and sophistication is just making matters worse and further diminishing faith in the leaders amongst the community.*

- **Lack of support / trust / credibility:** *So I've been out surveying opinions of leaders and media coverage and the biggest issues that have been emphasized is the "city's" and particularly Mayor Knowles and law enforcements lack of transparency regarding issues involving the shooting and complete disregard for addressing the racial tensions and lack of diversity.*

- **Poor choice of Words:** *Several people in the community and other elected officials discussed their concerns for the way Mayor Knowles and the city are handling things and how they are referring to people. Most said there is a lack of cultural sensitivity.*

- **Too much division:** *Everyone agreed that there could be more collaborations and that there was too much "my community" and "their community" going on when it came to elected officials, awareness and protesting campaigns, community organizations and etc...*

- **Need to change spokespeople:** *This may be the toughest piece but the consensus is that we either need to remove Mayor Knowles for a while or pair him up with some African American spokespeople to smooth some tensions. There was an overwhelming amount of comments that spoke to the lack of interest in supporting Mayor Knowles.*

Final Comments:

I hope everyone on both the agency and client side have thick skin and understand that none if this was meant to hurt feelings or to offend. We are dealing with a major issue here and we simply need to know where we are in terms of perceptions (to use as a benchmark) in order to be able to identify the appropriate strategies to overcome the barriers. If anyone has anything to add, take from this or whatever please chime in.

When we presented our update, we only received one response, not from anyone at the Partnership or Common Ground, and no one at the city either. It was just from Aaron Perlut:

Great update.

Later, I would learn that everyone else was personally offended by the e-mail, much like they were by my response to Aaron's "galvanizing moment" e-mail. The e-mail made them feel as though I was attacking them and their efforts, when I was just trying to get everyone on the same page. The black community and the community at large were the ones speaking. I was just the messenger.

CHAPTER 8

THE MAYORS OF NORTH COUNTY

"There is not a racial divide in the City of Ferguson."

Those words, spoken by the Mayor, felt like a slap in the face. They were a slap in the face to both the PR professional in me, who had lobbied so hard against the interview, and also to the young African-American male in me. They were like a knife in the back.

I saw Mayor Knowles digging his own grave on national television. It happened on MSNBC's *News Nation* with Tamron Hall. The two were conducting a remote interview, and, as far as I could tell, Ms. Hall was about to leap through the television screen and put the Mayor in a chokehold.

I could've easily gone and finished the job for her.

After all of the protests, rioting, public demonstrations and outcries, the Mayor was now claiming that there was absolutely no racial tension. There was overwhelming evidence to discredit his claim, and yet, he *still* continued to deny that anyone was upset about it. That's how big his ego was at the time. He was willing to do *anything* for self-preservation.

Then, it got worse.

Tamron Hall belted him across national airwaves. She asked, "Is that *your* perspective, or do you believe that is the perspective of African-Americans in your community?"

"That is the perspective of all residents in our city."

Not only did he claim to have that view, but also claimed that all 22,000 residents were on the same page. I thought this man was deluded.

"With all due respect," Ms. Hall responded, "Are you *listening* to them?"

In all my time in Ferguson, I had been wondering the same thing. I had never fully connected with the Mayor. I had never been able to gauge whether he truly knew his community. Now, I knew that he did not.

It was hurtful to me as a black man, and also hurtful as someone who had been going out into the community *every night* and strategizing with the affected people--a large portion of those 22,000 that the Mayor spoke of. The black community had made it known loud and clear that they did not consider Mayor Knowles a true leader. The fact that he didn't care, and didn't show to care, was nothing other than a reinforcement of their feelings. As a black man, these peoples' struggle was my own; it was something I could truly relate to, and it was something that the mayor had openly admitted to me that he could not. Why then, was he saying the complete opposite when the door was open for him to start constructive conversation? Was it because he thought that if he said it enough times, it would become true? Was it because he was severely deluded? Was it because he was an up-and-coming Republican politician, and any blemish on his city would be a blemish on his record?

He didn't need to give the public any more reasons to hate him. This interview was a blemish that dug his grave, and put the nail in the coffin.

As the interview went on, the mayor's stoic face became anxious and sweaty, as he stumbled over his words in front of the entire country.

At this point in time, the mayor wasn't the one I was most angry with. After all, I should have known he would have found a way to mess it up somehow. In my eyes, the real offender was Common Ground. They were too eager with the media, even after the chaos following the release of the alleged robbery video. Their only strength was getting spokespeople booked on air. Whether it was CNN, MSNBC or Fox, they'd sign the mayor up and throw him into the spotlight. They wouldn't even try to identify the direction of the narrative, didn't prep the Mayor for culturally and racially specific questions, or assess the impact their interviews would have on the black community if things went wrong. A seasoned, multicultural PR firm considers all of those things.

I kept telling them, "The Mayor and Chief are small-time guys. They don't know how to handle the national spotlight. They haven't been properly trained for this level of interviewing. If they go on-air with award-winning journalists, they *will* get eaten alive."

Because their interviews and word choices continued to ignite flames, I needed them to step out of the way. I said, "Take two weeks off. Get out of town. Get the Mayor and the Chief out of town while I work on the strategy. We may not be able to do anything about the fire given the situation, but at least you won't be adding any kerosene."

They didn't care. Booking media interviews was their specialty, so if they weren't doing that, then they weren't doing anything. What else were they expected to do? They didn't want to have to go into the city like us, in the eye of the storm, and get their coats wet with urine and spit. They had no sense of cultural awareness, and didn't want to listen to us. For all they cared, they were perfectly happy with my firm doing the dirty work on the streets to develop a real plan, while they relaxed in St. Louis like Elasticity, booking more and more interviews.

As the Mayor was finishing up, my phone buzzed in my pocket. It was an e-mail from Megan, the City Clerk, letting me know that a meeting had been scheduled with the rest of the mayors of North County. This was called 'The 24:1 Meeting'.

I then received an e-mail from Denise. They'd just booked the Mayor for a radio interview later that night.

It was just ridiculous.

THE 24:1 MEETING

The concept of 24:1 started from a years-old initiative with the simple goal of uniting the 24 municipalities of North County for collective prosperity. The goal was to create one collective vision for all 24 municipalities. Periodically, all of the mayors from those 24 municipalities would meet to discuss taxes, tourism, community, and appropriations of the region's funding.

Obviously, today's meeting had considerably different implications than the previous ones, and that's why I was invited to go. I wanted to arrive at the meeting before the Mayor so that I could buy him a little recovery time, since he was double-booked for media interviews by Common Ground.

On the way to the meeting, I said, "This is the dumbest Mayor I've ever worked with." I leaned my head back, closed my eyes, and took a deep breath. I knew that the Mayor was culturally incompetent, but so were most of the white residents of the area. They carried a very odd mentality that was oblivious to any racial tension.

When I arrived at the meeting, I just took a seat in the back of the room, watching everyone else talk about the interview. I heard people say things like, "Stupid Republican," and "What a dumbass." I heard a few folks comment on how he was a young hotshot with a hot head. What most people agreed on, though, was that Mayor Knowles had done a good job of screwing it up for the rest of them.

One official said, "I've watched him every year since he's been a mayor. If anyone could mess up an interview like that, I knew it'd be him."

"Same here," one of the mayors said. The two of them slapped hands. A few others joined in.

I couldn't believe the mayor bashing that was going on. Weren't these meetings supposed to be about unity? I guess it didn't help that I agreed with them.

Just then, the Mayor walked through the door. Chris straightened his tie, turned away from me, and stood up.

"Knowles, how's it going, my man?" he said. The two did a handshake hug like a couple of fraternity brothers. Patrick Green, the mayor of Normandy, said, "What's happenin', James?" and a few others behind him said something similar.

In a matter of moments, the conversations of Mayor Knowles had drastically changed. Suddenly, he represented a tragic hero, and no one had more guts than he did for sticking through it all.

Knowles only smiled as he shook the hands of others. If only he had heard what they really thought of him. If only these meetings were transparent. Maybe then, he would be able to stop all of his egotism and convince himself that he didn't need to do any more interviews.

He finally made his way to me. I stood up and he shook my hand. "Devin, how are you, buddy?" He smiled even wider, and I couldn't help thinking that even though he said my name, he was speaking to everyone else, like he was showing off his "black friend" in front of the whole meeting.

The words, *there's not a racial divide*, flashed through my mind.

"Devin," he said, "There are a few people I want you to meet. This is Chris Krehmeyer. He's the organizer of these meetings."

I flashed him a weak smile, and he did the same. Behind him, I felt the eyes of the other mayors staring straight at me. They knew I had heard everything they said, but they had no idea I was there as a consultant with Mayor Knowles.

THE GOVERNOR STRUGGLES TO RELATE

At another North County mayors meeting, Governor Jay Nixon showed up, in an effort to commune with the mayors who were being affected by the unrest. His intentions, he stated, were to relate to the community better. He didn't really do much relating at all, though. In fact, he spent most of the time talking when he should have been listening.

I sat in the back once again, and listened to him regurgitate nonsense about relationships, and how important it was for us to "stick together" as representatives of the people. You would have thought he was running for president, it was such a political speech. I looked around the room and noted the skepticism on every mayor's face.

The governor went on, telling us that he and others were trying their best, and that he has listened to stories from his African-American friends. He even said, "I can relate to Felons, we have them working at the mansion".

I looked around once again. I just knew that the black leaders in the room were ready to explode. Had Senator Rita Days been there, she would have been outraged. She spoke her mind. She was a diamond, the only real one in a sea of cubic zirconias. But none of the leaders said a word. They kept a straight face for their Governor, like what he just said was fine and dandy. But I didn't answer to anyone in that room. I had questions, and I needed answers.

I stood up and said, "Excuse me, Governor." The governor stopped. He looked surprised that anyone else was talking, or that anyone else was in the room for that matter. To him, he was reciting a pre-written speech, and he might as well have been talking to a wall. In reality, he was lost somewhere in a prewritten speech and could not find a way to get back on track. He was horrible, and everyone on my side of the room snickered and suggested he was either drunk or high.

"Yes sir," he said, "Mr. . ."

"Devin James," I said, "Governor, I can't sit by without addressing the disconnect in government here."

The Governor ruffled through a stack of papers in front of him, and he cut me short.

"Devin James?" He said, "I'm not finding your name listed here. Which municipality are you here representing?"

"What do you mean?"

"Well, I assume you're here as a mayor?"

I had been in nearly half a dozen meetings with the Governor, including multiple events at the Governor's mansion where I was repeatedly photographed with him and the first lady. I had even personally invited him to various non-profit charitable events around town and in Kansas City, and had worked with the Partnership to develop talking points for him in the past. Suddenly, he didn't know that I wasn't a mayor.

I said, "You talk about unity, but you don't even know which of us are mayors? I'm not a mayor; I'm the communications expert hired to assist the City of Ferguson.'"

But the governor wasn't fazed at all. He just stacked his papers once again, cut me off and said, "I'm sorry, this isn't your time to talk. This is a meeting for mayors."

I interrupted, "But the Mayor I'm representing has no idea what to ask for, he doesn't know what the city needs are for this type of situation, he's here to…"

He cut me off once more and said, "You need to sit down."

After a brief verbal scuffle between the Governor and me, Hazel Irby, from St. Louis County Council District 1 came to my defense, and asked for both the governor and the mayors to hear me out, once all the mayors had spoken.

The Governor replied, sharply and frustrated, "Well, I have nothing to do with that. You guys can talk all you want when I leave."

I took my seat thinking, "this is a meeting for mayors," he said. If that were the case, you'd think he would have at least let *them* and their representatives speak.

CHAPTER 9

TANKS AND BRACELETS

AT THIS POINT, my team understood that both city officials and the police department needed to acknowledge their role in; the institutional racism that plagued the black community and the death of Michael Brown. Then identify the steps to remedy the organizational and policy issues, and put together a community engagement plan to reconcile with "all" the members of its community. Unfortunately, the ingredients of effective communication were all missing. The people I worked with were neither transparent nor humble. They did not divulge any of their incriminating information to me willingly. Instead, they presented themselves as scapegoats of something that they themselves were not responsible for.

They covered up details and pretended that major problems didn't exist. That made it impossible for me to do my job.

One notable cover-up that I discovered was the presence of military-grade weapons in Ferguson. Again and again, I was assured that the Ferguson Police Department did not have any military-grade equipment. In fact, many officials went on record with the media saying the same thing. It made sense. After all, why and where would a small city of 22,000 house Humvees, tear gas, and riot equipment?

The video evidence didn't lie. There were Humvees, tear gas, and riot equipment being used in the Ferguson streets. If you were an uninformed viewer, you may have thought you were watching a scene in Baghdad or Kuwait. Law enforcement officials shouted through bullhorns, "Get off the streets! Return to your homes immediately". Cans of tear gas were thrown as a warning, and some officers even used rubber bullets on scattered civilians.

All of this was caught on video. Ferguson was a battlefield in the eyes of the media, but still, somehow, the police department and city officials were denying it.

I asked the Chief and City Manager many times if they possessed any of the military equipment, vehicles or riot gear, but I was never met with a clear answer. They repeatedly claimed that the equipment was being brought in by other, larger entities, but the city knew about it.

I said, "You should have been honest with the media, and especially with me. It's pointless to have a communications team here to help you explain things to the community and you're not being transparent."

They still wouldn't listen, and the riots kept going on, tarnishing Ferguson's reputation. Whether it was the National Guard, St. Louis County Police, Ferguson police, or outside law enforcement, they all used too much equipment and force.

At this point, the Partnership and some city officials saw me as a threat. They were hoping for me to come in, believe their story, and help the media and community understand their point of view. But that wasn't why I was there. I was there to empower the neglected black community and help rebuild the relationships between them and their local government. I was hired to find out what was wrong and figure out a way to change it, and that's what I was going to do. The black community wanted change, and I knew that it had to come from policy changes, not a spokesman swap. From that point, I made it my duty to both inspire and implement as many changes in the system as I could.

THE BRACELETS

In March 2015, the Department of Justice released the report of its investigation on the Ferguson Police Department. During the investigation, the Department discovered some terrible truths that had been covered up for many years. There were e-mails sent by city officials with racial slurs against Ferguson residents and against President Obama. There was clear evidence that the police force had targeted black residents. Despite Ferguson's being only 70% black, 93% of arrests made in Ferguson were of black residents. The report also showed the use of force was disproportionate to black residents, and that all uses of police canines were on black residents.

The report clearly had shown that deep-seated systemic racism existed in Ferguson, and that the officers were unwilling to admit it. The fact that the police force was only three percent black alone made it clear that there was a reason behind the disproportionate arrests. Over time, it became increasingly clear that there was a blatant disconnect between police and residents that needed to be addressed.

My firm and I met with Ferguson Assistant Chief of Police Al Eickhoff one afternoon to try to speak with him regarding details of any arrests, altercations or issues arising from the protests. He would not give us any information. It felt like we had this blackout period from the time we were with Chief Jackson to when Eickhoff's shift started. He was definitely anti-Devin, and it felt like he was anti-anything for the black community. He and Public Information Officer Tim Zoll seemed to be the biggest contributors to the lack of transparency on the departments end, because they were the worst at releasing information. I had established a respectable rapport with the Chief, but with the riots, lies, and cover-ups, I was hesitant to trust anyone else. I was much less inclined to trust the Assistant Chief.

As seen in many of the interviews, I found myself stationed at the city's police department while the rest of my team was stationed at City Hall. I worked every day out of the Chief's office, which he shared with the Assistant Chief. While in a meeting with the Chief, I was abruptly interrupted by one of the dispatchers who let me know that several media representatives were outside.

On one particular day, there were tons of reporters waiting in the hallway. They had somehow gotten inside the police station. I looked up and noticed Sharon Reed, whom I had been speaking with from KMOV. I walked with her and Art Holiday from KSDK down the hallway to discuss upcoming interviews.

Upon returning to the Chief's Office, I ended up sitting at the Assistant Chief's desk because the Chief had come back into the office. When I sat down, I noticed that he had a bracelet sitting on his desk. It was blue with white text, but I couldn't read it at first.

When Eickhoff walked in, I started explaining to him that there was value in transparency. The soldiers in the streets were counterproductive, and the fact they were lying about police involvement was even worse.

"You've already burned too many bridges in the community," I said. "It seems like every time I tell you guys something, you do the opposite of what I say. Every time you screw something up, you try to cover it up and only make things worse. I need you guys to start listening to me, and listening to the people, before you make any more decisions. Everything that goes out needs to come through me!"

"Look, Devin, it's our job to protect the residents, and that's exactly what we we're doing. Everything we do is about a measure of safety for Ferguson residents."

Law enforcement and government officials had a habit of using the word "residents" when they really meant "white residents." The Old Ferguson -- white Ferguson, was afraid that the blacks, or New Ferguson -- were coming in and taking over. They wanted to protect themselves, the true "residents" of Ferguson. The word was never used in reference to the black population.

I said, "But the black community is feeling more threatened than safe. This is just as much about public perception as it is about safety. Black people are trying to be heard, and when you use force against them, they feel like they're being marginalized."

Eickhoff moved some stuff on his desk to grab a folder. He left the drawer open, and inside I could see a box full of the same blue bracelets.

By now my curiosity had gotten the best of me. I reached over and grabbed the bracelet on his desk and turned it over. It said, "I am Darren Wilson."

I signaled to my assistant to look at the bracelets sitting on the desk. She wrote on her note pad next to her, "WTF!" with a look of pure confusion.

She and I stood up, shook our heads in disgust, and walked out of the room. We speculated for a while. To me, wearing and supporting these bracelets not only showed loyalty to a homicidal policeman, but it also mocked the "I am Mike Brown" campaign. It was like a playground come-back, shoving a proverbial middle finger at the people who were peacefully supporting the other side.

I talked to the Chief about the bracelets. I never told him that I saw Eickhoff with them in his drawer. The Chief said he was not aware of the bracelets, but firmly asserted that he did not support anyone wearing them, ever. Sergeant Harry Dilworth, an African-American, and the other black officers agreed.

But don't think because Sergeant Dilworth is black that he's good for the black community. He harassed Orlando Brown after listening to him in a meeting with the Chief and myself. Brown maintained that Dilworth put a warrant out for his arrest after he refused to help clear the 300-plus-member crowd at the meeting. According to Brown, Dil-worth said, "Lock his ass up!" after Brown refused to clear the large crowd. Brown contended that Dilworth only knew his name because of his writing it down at the meeting I hosted. Brown maintained that Dilworth was angry with protestors in general, but took his frustrations out on Brown personally. This was another violation of trust.

FERGUSON'S THERAPIST

Imagine going into a therapist's office to get help working through a personal issue. You lay down on his couch, and the therapist gets out his notebook and starts asking you questions. Instead of answering them, however, you get insecure and scared that the therapist will judge you. Instead of talking, you keep your mouth shut for the whole session. Week after week, you come back, and each time, you say absolutely nothing. Then, after months of doing this, you sit up and ask the therapist why you haven't had any results.

"Well, you haven't been open with me," the therapist would say.

"Yes, but I've been paying you money. You haven't done your job," you would say.

Then, the therapist would say, "That's because you haven't allowed me to do so."

In Ferguson, I was the therapist, and the Ferguson officials were the patients. Just like the example, the officials were unwilling to talk. If they had been open, and trusted me to do my job, the results would have been amazing. We could have avoided many of the blunders, chaos and damage because we could have taken a step back to have compassion. But they were on the defense and were too insecure to admit to any wrongdoings. I did my best to do my job, but they did their best to prevent me from being able to do that.

It only got worse from there.

CHAPTER 10

CLAYTON PROTESTS

THE PROTESTS ON AND near West Florissant Avenue were gaining attention worldwide. Videos of the demonstrations were being shared on Facebook, Reddit, and other social media sites. This proved to be valuable to the people of Ferguson, because it served as a source of support from people all of the world, who otherwise would not have heard of this small town in St. Louis County.

The only problem was that the chants weren't reaching the people in charge. On a basic level, many of the demonstrations were just preaching to the choir. The people near West Florissant Avenue were already on board. People on the Internet were jumping on board. The people in power were the only ones who were unmoved.

The protests occurred around the time when the grand jury was meeting to decide whether to indict Darren Wilson. Bob McCullough, the prosecuting attorney for St. Louis County, was the man who chose to bring Darren Wilson's case before a grand jury instead of bringing charges himself. McCullough had only brought cases before a grand jury a handful of times in his career, and each time, the defendant was not indicted. He also made the decision before the investigation was over.

The African-American community was both outraged and threatened by McCulloch's presence on the case. Many people called for the governor to remove him from the case, since his father was a law enforcement officer who was killed on duty by a black man. He had a history of letting policemen off easy and had never brought charges against policemen who had killed black men.

The decision to keep McCullough on the case was a display of carelessness and insensitivity within both the county and state government. Once again, the decision showed the ingrained marginalization of the black community in Ferguson. We were not being heard, or even considered. The protesters knew this, and were fed up. They decided to move into Clayton, where Bob McCullough's office was located.

Clayton sits southwest of Ferguson, and is the county seat of St. Louis County. It holds all of the most important governmental and economic offices in the county. Its demographic makeup is 78% white and only 8% black, a stark contrast to the surrounding municipalities.

MOVING INTO CLAYTON

Around mid-day, dozens of people started showing up outside of Clayton's Buzz Westfall Justice Center with picket signs, megaphones, and t-shirts displaying Michael Brown's picture. They began chanting and singing songs, like "No Justice, No Peace" and "Hands Up, Don't Shoot." A dozen policemen arrived outside the building and zip-tied the front doors shut so that none of the protesters could get inside. The officers called the protests a threat to the city's safety.

The policemen took their places in front of the building to further protect the property from being destroyed, even though it was a peaceful protest. At one point, the crowd became hostile, and the people were warned not to cross the police line. It was ridiculous because, on any other given day, the people would have been free to assemble and even enter the building. But because the black community was protesting, the police barred them from entry. A few patrons defied the orders and stepped over the police line. They were immediately arrested.

The crowd left before nightfall but promised that they would return and keep demonstrating. Over the next several days, more and more people came to help. The demonstrations then started spreading throughout the rest of Clayton.

The protesters had promised to disrupt business as usual in North County. Now, it seemed, they were actually doing it. Businesses around town closed their doors and refused to open. They were afraid that these people were going to start rioting and looting. They lumped the peaceful people into the same group as the violent people, simply because they were related to Ferguson. Even though the demonstrators had been completely peaceful, fear was high, and that proved to be the deciding factor.

A few days into the protest, I received a call from Aaron Perlut, who was at Elasticity's office in downtown St. Louis. He told me that the people at the Partnership were afraid that the protesters were going to damage the buildings in Clayton. They wanted Elasticity to come help them out, since they were supposed to be working in Ferguson and knowledgeable about the riots and protest. But Elasticity hadn't been doing anything in Ferguson, so Aaron came to me.

"They're in Clayton because they're angry at McCullough," I said, "No one is trying to hear them out in Ferguson, so they're going where people will pay attention to them."

Elasticity had never even set foot in Ferguson. Now, Aaron wanted to pull me away from my work so I could help them out, as if they were in some sort of mortal danger. There wasn't anything I could do to help them, though, because to me, they weren't in danger at all.

I also thought it interesting that the Partnership felt the need to summon the only black contractor they had away from his work to handle a mostly minority crowd. I wondered what made the white community fear blackness so much in that moment. To me, the experience spoke to the level of ignorance that both the white community and business leaders in Clayton had towards progressive race relations. No one wanted to sit down and discuss real issues. The first line of offense was pretending the storm wasn't there, not walking through it to see greater results.

It was not the first time that I was defiant when it came to Elasticity or the Partnership. But I was fully justified. Why was it that when protesters were making their mark in Ferguson, officials sat back, letting the fire burn? They didn't care at all until it was in their neighborhoods and business districts. But suddenly, when they were threatened, it became a real issue of safety. The experience showed that Ferguson officials did not take the Ferguson demonstrations seriously. One protest group told my team of their interest in taking the protest to Frontenac, Maryland Heights and other affluent and upper middle-class cities to shake things up, but they were scared they would face some very real dangers because white cops in those areas were already on high alert.

THE RESULT

The protestors could wave signs and picket all they wanted, but it wouldn't do much more than disrupt "business as usual." As soon as the people left, the businesses started re-opening.

Unfortunately, Clayton won the battle. Governor Nixon did not exercise his authority to remove McCullough from the case. McCullough is known for defending the police, and stepping down from this case would cause a blow to his reputation amongst the conservative community. Consequently, he would also risked losing the support of the police force too. If the Governor had exercised his authority to remove McCullough from the case, it would have created two completely different beliefs regarding his decision. On one hand, he would have been heralded for removing such a biased attorney from the case. On the other hand, his colleagues in government—from police officers to conservative officials—would have derided him for bucking under the pressures of society, and undermining the law by removing an otherwise "competent" figure (and long-time attorney) from a particular case. He would be called "soft" by his peers, and looked at as a government figure unable to stand his ground. The reasons behind the decision to keep McCullough on the case were purely political, and as such, Darren Wilson's trial would start without the most needed consideration: justice.

The grand jury went into session, and took two months to come to a decision. All the while, the protesters were helpless to stop it.

CHAPTER 11

WHEN ALL WHITE AIN'T RIGHT

AN INTERESTING PHENOMENON happens when a media storm hits. First, there's the story itself. Then, there's the public reaction and commentary on that story. For the African-American population in Ferguson, the public reaction was one of distress, anger, and cynicism. The commentary was one of skepticism, mockery, and laughter.

Usually, after only a few days, though, there comes a point when the story and its commentary is no longer fresh or exciting to anyone who is not immediately involved. At this point, the media starts scraping towards the bottom of the barrel. In essence, it begins a cycle of stories within the story. Then, there is more reaction, and more commentary, and it starts all over again.

That's not to say that the death of Brown was the only story worth covering. The ensuing riots and protests were all part of that first tier as well, and they all deserved the same amount of attention. But another big "story within a story" to hit Ferguson came on August 18. PRNewser, a news blog, had "supposedly" done some digging on Common Ground PR, and had discovered that the firm was 100% female, and 100% white.

The PRNewser article writer went on a rant, noting that while Common Ground may be a professional firm with great credentials, the simple fact that there were no minority staff working on their team in Ferguson indicated that they were not the right fit for the job.

Soon, other media outlets began picking up on the story. PRNewsOnline wrote,

> In the wake of the racial tensions that have engulfed Ferguson following the fatal shooting of Michael Brown, the City might have considered expanding its PR tent to bring in more diverse communications agencies, maybe even a black-owned PR firm. Isn't a broader perspective exactly what the people who run Ferguson need? If Common Ground really has only white folks on its team, it begs the question whether the City recognizes the severity of the situation.

As is the case with most blogs these days, many of these articles were written in a patchwork manner. This means that the "reporters" aren't actually doing any research, but rather, they're basing their findings on hearsay from other media outlets. Then, they voice their own opinions. Once just *one* of those articles catches fire, those opinions become the news, and in effect, become "the facts" to the public.

The fire had spread, and within 24 hours, the story was plastered on Twitter and Instagram. Twitter commenters began railing against Common Ground, Ferguson, and the city management all over again. By the end of August 19, Common Ground had taken over the top headline.

I didn't really mind. After all, the media was reclaiming what I had already made clear: that Common Ground was unfit to advise Ferguson officials on how to help solve issues in the black community. The only difference is that the media still had no clue *how* unfit they truly were.

The PRNewser article further stated, "Given this situation, the firm could be totally qualified to handle a big media relations project. But . . . with race a big factor in this case, choosing a firm so lacking in diversity is eye catching."

Personally, I knew that they were not only unfit from a racial and cultural standpoint, but also from a professional standpoint. Their media strategy in Ferguson thus far (to book any media outlet we can get, which continued even *after* the Tamron Hall debacle) proved that they were never intent on helping Ferguson with its issues. Instead, they only wanted to look busy, to receive some notoriety for taking the assignment, and to get paid.

THE SHOW CONTRACT

In an attempt to show the media and their peers that they were not culturally insensitive, Denise instructed Ferguson officials to draw up a contract with the purpose of adjoining the Devin James Group as a minority subcontractor. Up to that point, my firm and I felt as though we had been marginalized for the sake of the other firms' interests. The contract was drawn up, and released to the media. Here's a snippet of our agreement:

> *DJG shall provide such services necessary to develop a community engagement plan and strategy and work with the City with regard to the implementation of such Plan. The specific services of the consultant are described in the proposal, attached hereto as Exhibit A.*

> *CGPR shall provide services to interact with the media on behalf of the City, handle media requests, and consult with City officials and staff concerning media appearances and interaction. The specific services of the consultant are described in the proposal, attached hereto as Exhibit B.*

Despite not having a plan in place after more than a week since the death of Michael Brown, Common Ground's main focus was getting this contract executed to save face in the PR community. The Partnership was in on this, too, as Katy was the one who recommended that I work with Common Ground. Since we hadn't officially gotten a contract with the Partnership for the new "Ferguson black community engagement" work, they worked it out with the Ferguson City Manager for my firm to receive a $5,000 deposit payment that was meant to offset initial setup expenses (but would later be deducted from my budget/contract with the Partnership).

THE COST OF INFORMATION

I was shocked. Once again, the firm that many (including myself) held in high regard was proving its extreme inept-ness. It became painfully apparent that no one I had met was being truly transparent, and that not one of the Common Ground team members had the cultural competence to even process what was going on. Their thoughts were on their reputations and their pockets, and that was only the begin-ning.

For the most part, the research aspect of our "Community Engagement Plan" did not involve the city at all, but did in-volve reviewing city and police department documents. We soon found out that once the barrage of sunshine requests came into City Hall, documents started being re-filed, al-tered, or deleted altogether.

A few months down the line, I would speak with Jason Leopold, an investigative reporter for *Vice News*. He told me that he had been following Ferguson, and wanted to see what was going on inside the city for himself. Like so many other reporters, he made a sunshine request. When the ad-ministrators got back to him a few days later, he was informed that he would need to pay for the request, due to the bulk that they were receiving at the time.

Jason said, "Fine. I'll shell out a little bit of money."

In the end, he spent over $2000 for City Hall to process the request. When Jason received the documents a few days lat-er, he realized that a lot of information was missing.

There were e-mail chains where I could tell that e-mails were missing. There were gaps in the dates, and there were gaps in the conversations on important topics. None of that added up. I found a chain of e-mails between you and the administrators, and it all showed that they were not listening to you.

But if you knew what Megan and Stephanie were doing inside City Hall, it added up perfectly. The high price tag was implemented not only to bring in money for the city, but also to discourage as many people as possible from making sunshine requests. The edits and deletions were made so that even if you did pay for a request, you wouldn't find anything incriminating about the city or its workers. It created an endless cycle; if the media couldn't learn the truth about what was going on, they wouldn't have the facts needed to spur more sunshine requests. It was a highly unethical violation of the Freedom of Information Act, and it was done intentionally.

DEAR ANONYMOUS

In August 2014 Ferguson's City Hall had been allegedly hacked by the "hacktivist" group Anonymous. I can't say I know for sure it was them, but someone had taken down the city's web server, and tried to gain access to classified information. This was a key moment, because it meant that everyone in City Hall had to communicate offline. The experience gave my team and me our first look into the paperwork that showed how insensitive Ferguson had been for years and years. If it weren't for the Anonymous efforts, we wouldn't have seen half the paperwork we did, and I would have been steering much more blindly.

MOVING IN

Even though our initial assignment in Ferguson was to develop a community engagement—and not to handle communications or public/media relations—we realized that we would not be able to do anything when Common Ground, Elasticity and the Partnership were taking the city and the black community three steps back for every step forward.

When my firm and I discovered that Common Ground was doing practically nothing at all to help develop a better communication strategy for the city to address the people, we essentially kicked them out of the Natta Room and took it over. Remember this, though, from the moment we asserted ourselves, we were trying to implement a moment of silence. We knew what we were doing, and the only thing they knew was how to set up tons of unneeded media interviews. Based on their definition of community engagement, they were looking for us to host job fairs, block parties, picnics and carnivals to distract people. That was ridiculous; there was no cause for a "celebration," so I wasn't going to play any games with my community. Consequently, we told them to get out.

It wasn't a harsh goodbye, either. Common Ground wanted out. They had only joined the account so they could have the reputation of being the firm that "fixed Ferguson." They had no idea of the kind of work that actually needed to be done. At some point, there were alleged confidential conversations about all the firms, and I emerged as one who didn't need their help. This conversation sparked tension between Denise and me, and eventually, we stopped speaking altogether.

The Natta Room would become our home at City Hall over the next few months. My team and I slept in those chairs more than we slept in our own beds, but even then, it was only for a few hours a night. When we weren't at City Hall, we were at the police station or back out in the streets, meeting with representatives from local protest groups, community members, youth and even local gangs. We were learning what their concerns were, and documenting them, so that we could both convey their feelings effectively to the city officials and ensure their feedback was included in the planning.

FERGUSON TAKES A BACK SEAT

Even though protests had not been violent the previous night, tensions were high as the grand jury investigation began on Darren Wilson. On the previous morning, Michael Brown's parents, Michael Brown Sr. and Lesley McSpadden, went on the *Today Show*. Although their words were few, they made it clear that the only way to return peace to Ferguson was for Wilson to be tried and convicted. The key word they used was "justice."

The community knew that it could take weeks, or even months, for the jury to come to a decision, and despite Michael Brown Sr.'s assurance that justice would be served, many were skeptical that Wilson would be brought to trial especially after McCullough refused to recuse himself. The fact that the media was not allowed in the jury hearings made it all worse, as they could only speculate on what was happening behind the closed doors. Collectively, the black community began to hold its breath.

On August 20th at noon, I received an e-mail from Denise regarding her "comeback" article. We hadn't spoken since I kicked Common Ground out of the Natta room, and had only communicated sporadically through project management software my firm set up to help manage all of the chaotic and unorganized communications that were stifling our efforts. I was caught off-guard when she asked me for a favor in her e-mail:

> Hey Devin - can you take a peek at this? With your input, I'll share with John and send to PR Week, O'Dwers, etc. Should I say that in the coming days you will be announcing what that going forward program will look like?
>
> Can you offer language for that?
>
> Thanks!
> Denise

Attached was a Word document, apparently drafted by Denise herself earlier that day. It was a press release that she intended to provide to the news outlets--many of which had spoken recklessly about her firm. In the document, she stated:

> Just as an EMT would respond to a 911 call, Common Ground PR offered immediate, emergency help in the form of fielding the overwhelming number of media inquiries the City was receiving until it assembled a long term team to handle this crisis.

The article was long and full of empty rhetoric, claiming that Common Ground had joined the Ferguson effort out of the goodness of its heart. Denise was deflecting every claim

126

that her firm was not fit for the job. But their defensiveness was obvious:

> *I was dismayed at the negative reaction online and on social media, especially among fellow communications professionals, who pointed at the lack of diversity on our staff as a sign of the "greater problem." Increasing the diversity of communications professionals is an industry-wide challenge that we all need to tackle. But as a local St. Louisan who watched this tragedy unfold, I offered our assistance because it was clear that this community was overwhelmed and needed immediate help fielding media inquiries. The color of our skin reflected nothing of our concern to help our broader community respond to the watchful world.*

I was shocked to read this, in part because of its intentions. So far, I had nothing positive to say about Common Ground, and they knew that. They knew that I thought they were garbage, even though I hadn't said it. So why, then, was the CEO of the PR firm voted "Best of St. Louis" coming to me for advice on a press release? Did she not feel competent in addressing the industry herself? Was her team not suited for their own PR nightmare?

This was a huge wake-up call. It reminded me of how much trash was in the PR business and that all of the accolades, awards and trophies are worthless. If you can afford to pay membership fees to join all the associations, take the classes, attend the meetings and pay the registration fees at all the conferences, your firm could be an award-winning PR firm, too!

To Denise's credit, the article itself was sophisticated, professional, and had some great buzzwords. Unfortunately, however, Denise was missing the entire point once again.

Common Ground was coming under scrutiny for having an all-white staff and lacking cultural connections. It was another cultural lashing of Ferguson, all while the black community was angry. An all-white firm in the center of a black-white racial conflict is incorrect when the white community acts as the aggressor. She could not possibly expect the black community to tolerate the fact that her firm, a white firm, was sent in to "save Ferguson" from the calamities endured at the hands of white people. She didn't understand that this time, her color had everything to do with it. Black people can't be heard through white ears—whites in Ferguson needed to listen to black viewpoints and black thoughts. This particular bout of criticism just happened to come at her instead of another white firm, but she couldn't say that she didn't place herself into the fire. Whether she thought it was fair or not was no longer relevant. From a public relations standpoint, she would only be burying herself deeper if she released this as a comeback to the public outcry.

Her article went on to further explain that she *had* partnered with a minority PR firm, and she was happy to announce it to the world:

> In my first conversation with Ferguson City officials, I advised that any solution to strife and development of long-term reconciliation would have to come with the assistance of a member of the black community skilled at community engagement with these key constituents.
>
> To that end, The Devin James Group has also been serving St. Louis County and the City of Ferguson to be an independent liaison to handle the long-term needs, work with community leaders and seek regional support in a grassroots effort to build

true engagement. With the long-term coalition and communications help of CEO Devin James, local residents and businesses can focus on determining what's best for this community.

To any casual onlooker, you would have thought I'd have been flattered, but behind the scenes, Denise had not even spoken to me in the week beforehand. This lack of communication, coupled with mentioning me in a press release, made it clear that she was not being sincere. However, I am a team player at all times, and as such, I kept my cool. At the time, I wasn't certain what level of involvement any of these "firms" would have later on, but I took special note to remember the power dynamics of the situation. Even though I was being sought out for my "expertise and cultural connections," I still ultimately had no power in the inner circles, and I didn't want to be exiled before I could even get anything done for my community. In a game-time decision, I provided her with some revisions. She stuck them in her document, and hit save.

Within a half an hour, the article was written to Denise's satisfaction, and she copied me on an e-mail to Ferguson City Manager John Shaw with the article attached:

John – I need to respond to stories running in my professional media about Common Ground and would like to share the following with them. This is crucial for my clients and employees to see me defend why we agreed to assist. Devin has reviewed as well.

Your earliest review is greatly appreciated! We will send this to PRNews, PRWeek and O'Dwyers Media.

The last e-mail annoyed me the most. During all this tur-moil, it seemed that Denise *needed* to respond to these stories railing against her firm. Never mind the myriad of stories that were railing against the very client she was hired to help. I continued to be surrounded by people who were only concerned with themselves.

FUNDING THE FIRE

Denise released the article to the listed news outlets that very day. She probably sent them within an hour of our e-mail exchange, because it was up and posted online by the end of the day.

As predicted, however, the response from the public was not positive. Even PR firms chimed in on social media to say that they were not pleased with Common Ground's handling of their own crisis.

On August 22, matters became worse when several media outlets started reporting that Common Ground had set up a crowd-funding page for Darren Wilson. She denied this to me and sent a text that she had heard Ferguson Public In-formation Officer (PIO) Tim Zoll had done it.

This was a horrible PR strategy, and I don't think that it ever would have hit social media if Common Ground hadn't retaliated to the initial accusations of being insensitive to mi-norities. The fact that they chose to write back meant that the name Common Ground was now in the public domain of consciousness. Suddenly, it wasn't just "Ferguson and their PR firm," it was "the all-white PR firm Common Ground."

The next day would be the first time Denise and I came into contact since the press release three days before. She sent me a text message at 9:44 a.m., with a screenshot of what others had been tweeting and a text that read:

I think it will help understanding on social media if you could tweet back on a few of these, reinforcing DJG engagement and our relationship. Thoughts?

If it wasn't clear already, it became clearer that Denise's heart was not in Ferguson for the right reasons. She had other priorities, and it involved keeping her own brand separate from all the racial issues that her own client had shown. Most importantly, she was concerned with everyone's opinion of her, and by everyone, I mean everyone who was white in her circles. She was worried about the impact this was having on her other clients, and the fact she was once the media's darling and now she was in unfamiliar space.

I wouldn't have been able to stop the storm if I tried. Common Ground was using the same strategy that they had been using all along for the Mayor and Chief—the mantra that any media is good media, and to respond to everything. Again, they were trying to put out a bonfire with kerosene. I didn't think it was a good strategy, but at this point, I was fed up with the firm. I could have helped her more, but Denise's personal fire was not my concern. I had an entire community's problems to deal with.

CHAPTER 12

ANDERSON COOPER

On August 21, my team and I were near the QuickTrip that had been looted and burned to the ground. In the community, this spot is known as Ground Zero.

My team hired a camera crew to follow us around on most days and nights. Our goal was to capture conversations with the locals in Ferguson: store owners, protesters, workers, unemployed, homeless, students, youth, etc. We wanted to capture this so that we could show Ferguson officials and the partnership what changes needed to be made in a way that they wouldn't think it was coming from me. I wanted to mostly hear from the people who weren't being heard above the national media. It was important for me to compile my information in a video format because I wanted to display raw testimonies of the people in the community. I wanted to showcase the things that weren't being said on TV—musings from the mouths of Ferguson residents themselves.

I was interviewing a young African-American woman in her early twenties who was working a local event. She hadn't been involved in any of the protests (but her white co-workers who went overboard trying to single her out had still distressed her). They didn't have bad intentions, but were insensitive to the effect that Mike Brown's death had on the young lady. In an interview, she told us:

> *They said, things like, 'You're not like the others. You're one of the good ones. You're a white black girl.' They made me feel as though I was special despite being black, like I had overcome some huge obstacle. In reality, it didn't make me feel special at all. I felt like I was stupid. It made me feel ashamed that they didn't think my race lived up to their standards. It made me feel like, before they got to know me, they saw me as just another black bitch, like they called the others.*

I've always found it interesting how low our standards are in this country. Right now, people respect me. I am dressed in a suit and tie, and I am clean-shaven. They refer to me as "Mr. James." That's how people treat me, like I'm one of the "good ones" that the young woman described. The instant I'm back in my jeans or gym clothes, I get pulled over, I get profiled, I get harassed and viewed as another thug who's up to no good. It's a common theme in the black community, especially amongst black men. Both law enforcement and the media portray us as guilty until proven innocent, and if we're ever found innocent, we never achieve social exoneration.

I remember one night in North County when I was driving home from the gym in a rental car. I had just finished playing basketball. I was sweaty from the game and didn't have my coat on in the car (although it was below freezing outside, I was in my car, and so it didn't matter much to me.) When I was on the highway going through St. Ann, I was pulled over. The officer got out of his car and tapped on my window, even though it was already partway down.

"You look a little nervous, young man," he said, "Why are you sweating?"

"I'm on my way home from the gym," I said.

"Really? And whose car is this?"

Was he serious? "It's a rental. It's for my business," I said.

He didn't believe me. As a black man, I had been in this predicament many times before. Because I was a black man in a car with gym clothes, the officer's first thought was that I could not possibly own the vehicle that I was driving. In reality, I do not own a car and haven't owned one since 2007. I ride the metro-rail car, or ride my bike everywhere as part of my own way of reducing the carbon footprint and maintaining a healthy lifestyle. Due to the crazy scheduling and hectic meetings all over town, my team and I decided to rent cars. This dually eliminated personal car use and reduced the chances people would familiarize themselves with the cars we owned and attack us. So I am hardly ever driving, let alone driving a "nice" car. This was a compact car, the cheapest car in the rental lot. I was racially profiled in a compact car. There is a notion that black people can only get profiled in a "nice" car, but that night proved that theory to be incorrect. I suppose that any black person driving any kind of car through St. Ann, Missouri can be profiled at any time.

"Could you step out of the car?" he said.

"No," I responded. "I'll hand you my I.D., but I know my rights, and I'm not going to step out of the car."

I was shivering already because it was cold and I was wearing a tank top and shorts and was soaking wet, but the officer "thought" it was because I was nervous. "Step out of the car," he said. "That's an order."

He seemed overly aggressive from the time he walked up to my car, so I was nervous. As a black man you have to be extremely careful when interacting with law enforcement. Any gestures, comments or movements you make can cause the officer to "fear for his life" and shoot you. While I was nervous, I was still calculating every move to prevent my untimely death. As a black man, you also cannot appear too knowledgeable or confident. If you know your rights and don't appear to be bowing down to their authority, many law enforcement officers take it as an insult. There's an unspoken "how dare you talk back to me" mentality that many law enforcement officers have, so as a black man in that environment, one is constantly on eggshells.

Next, he all but forced me out of the car. I couldn't even grab my jacket, or he would have probably thought I was reaching for a gun and shot me. He grabbed my license from me and told me to get down on the ground while he searched my car.

"I do not consent to a search," I said. "This is ridiculous. You have no right to search this car!"

"Get down on the ground!" he yelled. "I could have you arrested right here!"

Then, I heard someone yell back from the police car, "Hold on a minute!" It was another officer, and he was jogging toward us now. He walked up to the first officer, took my I.D. from his hand, and studied it for a minute.

"Are you Devin James?"

I hesitated to respond because I didn't know where this was going given the current circumstances. But I reluctantly said yes.

"This is Devin James," he said to the other officer who had me on the ground. "He's the guy helping Tom (Chief Jackson). Get him off the ground and let him go."

He handed me my I.D., and just like that, I was free to go. The first officer walked back to his car without saying anything, and the second pulled me aside.

"Here," he said, "take my business card. If you ever have any problems, let me know."

"Yeah, I got a problem," I said. "I was harassed by this officer for no reason, I was told to get on the ground for no reason, and now you're letting me go because I'm Devin James who is working with Tom, Chief Tom Jackson in Ferguson. But what would have happened if I wasn't Devin James, working with Chief Tom Jackson in Ferguson?"

The officer didn't have a straight answer. He said, "I'm really sorry, Devin. I can't answer that but what I can say is all of us are not the same. I hope you realize that."

The officer's last statement was important because it is true. All police officers are truly not the same. All of them do not want to beat up black people and throw bogus charges on them. All of them don't want to oppress an entire community. However, the fact remains that if I weren't Devin James who was working with Chief Tom Jackson in Ferguson that night, I would have been arrested, and only God knows what else.

Even after the embarrassing episode, I didn't file a complaint. After all, I know more about how to get officers in trouble for inappropriate conduct than many people, but had

I done that, I would have eliminated my unrestricted access to law enforcement and I still had things to do for the black community. I avoided making an official complaint, but I advised Chief Jackson and Belmar at St. Louis County about the incident next time I saw the two of them together at a DOJ meeting.

What about all the other people who aren't Devin James? These officers make dozens of stops every night. If they hadn't recognized my name, I would have been another one of their black victims, much like I had been many times before in my life.

THE INTERVIEW

It's August 21, a little past 6:00 p.m. and we had just completed the interview schedule for the day. Upon checking the time and my e-mails I noticed an e-mail from Denise to the Mayor confirming an interview. I was upset because both Denise and the Mayor did whatever they wanted to do, constantly, when it came to the media. Neither person ever thought to consider the consequences.

We had less than an hour before the Mayor's next big interview.

Denise had scheduled Anderson Cooper for that night. I remember saying to my assistant on the way there, "I just do not know where his or her head is at." We got the details of the interview location, and my assistant and I dropped what we were doing, left our team to wrap up interviews and took off toward the Mayor's house. I was 100% sure the Mayor wasn't ready for Anderson Cooper.

We pulled up to the house and parked in the driveway. I shot a text to the Mayor that we were outside. When the Mayor got in the car with his wife, he looked like he was going to have a panic attack.

"You good, man?" I said.

He nodded, yes, but a pool of sweat dripped from his forehead when he did. I remembered I had a towel in my backpack so I reached in my backpack to get it and handed it to the Mayor. He blotted his face, and nearly soaked the entire thing.

"James, we must cancel this," I said. "You know you don't have to do this interview."

"It'll be fine," he said. "It's Anderson Cooper, not a federal trial."

"Yeah, but you're a mess. Look at you. We're not even on the set yet and you look nervous as shit."

"Don't worry about it," he responded.

"OK. Well, do you want to go over the talking points you and Denise developed?" I said.

"She didn't prepare any for me; she just booked the interview," he said.

I spent the rest of the car ride giving him tips on how to handle himself. I used the crisis forecasting method I mentioned earlier; in a haste I came up with as many tough questions as I could to keep him from any extra criticism that was coming his way. I knew Anderson Cooper, and this interview was going to be everything but friendly.

Every time we rounded another corner, he looked like he was going to vomit, and I knew he wasn't retaining anything I had to offer him. There were stopping points put up by the National Guard at every street corner on West Florissant Avenue. I had to get out of the car several times to show my credentials so we could get clearance to proceed with our unauthorized vehicle, but we finally made it to the small media tent outside the Public Storage lot on the corner of Florissant and Canfield.

There was Anderson Cooper himself, getting a quick touchup on his makeup. The area wasn't roped off, so the protesters could get close. Cooper was seen with different people walking by, as well as taking 'selfies' with onlookers.

I escorted Mayor Knowles to the tent and greeted Kari Pricher, AC360's editorial producer, and the CNN crew. The whole time, I was still thinking we should have cancelled. Mayor Knowles was a wreck, and if his prior interviews were any indication, he'd find a way to screw this one up, too. I just knew there was no way he would make it through this interview without a huge blunder.

In just a few minutes, Mayor Knowles and Anderson Cooper were standing toe-to-toe under the tent. I was standing next to Van Jones, CNN's political commentator, when I heard Cooper make a comment about how nice a day it was, and that the weather had been great lately. They were just making small talk, but this wasn't Anderson Cooper being nice; he was really just trying to get Mayor Knowles to take his guard down.

Pedestrians lined the street behind them, hoping to get a good view. The spotlights shone on both of their faces, revealing the sweat on the Mayor's face. We got the signal that we were about to go live, and Anderson jumped right out of the gate.

"You have a police force which has 50 white officers, 3 African-American officers, the community here is 67% African American. How can there not be a disconnect or a divide?"

The Mayor started on one of his many rambles. "Well, I think there are clear differences between us. There are things that we continue to work on, but in Ferguson, we always try to work on our shared values--the things that bring us together. Clearly, we've continued, and we need to continue more, obviously, to bring our residents who feel that way-- who feel disaffected or disconnected--to bring that into the fold."

"But I've heard you say you don't believe that any resident here believes that there's a racial divide."

"And maybe that was too strong of a statement. I obviously wanted to impress upon people that the majority of residents of Ferguson don't feel that way."

"But the majority of residents in Ferguson are African American, and they are being policed by a force that does not represent them in terms of race. And I'm not saying that race is the only criteria here--"

"But you're kind of making race the only criteria, though," he interrupted.

I turned away. I couldn't take it anymore. The minute the light turned on--hell, before that--it was obvious the Mayor was going to get grilled. And how did he respond? The same way he did any other time he got grilled--he got very, very defensive. And just like all the other times, which only made him look tone deaf to the feelings of the black community. Within two minutes, he was attempting to talk over Cooper, and it was impossible to distinguish their words. They looked like preschoolers in a fight. But the only person who had anything to lose was Mayor Knowles, and he was losing it fast.

Finally, Anderson Cooper asked him what he had been asked many times since the interview with Tamron Hall,

"Just bottom line; you don't believe there's a racial divide here?"

If the mayor had any moment to come clean, this was it.

Cooper was using his position to get a quick sound bite. And it worked. Instead of repenting, the mayor tried to skew his words into a halfway statement. "There are obviously people who feel disconnected, and we have got to reach out to them, no doubt."

All I could think was, if it was obvious, then why did it take him so long to admit it? I sighed, knowing millions of viewers were thinking the same thing.

Anderson Cooper thanked the mayor. The two shook hands as though there were never any verbal sparring. We unhooked the Mayor's microphone and headed for the car. Off set, the Mayor's wife convinced him that he had done a great job.

On the way back to the car, the Mayor tried talking to some of the protesters, but he looked foolish. They attacked him, asking why they never saw him on Florissant before, and why he was neglecting New Ferguson.

He talked to a few people, but they shouted over him and he left without giving them any answers. Trymaine Lee, a Pulitzer Prize-winning reporter for MSNBC, stopped us. Lee asked for an interview with the Mayor, and I granted it.

Meanwhile, the crowd of people behind him was growing, so I stepped in and cut the interview short. It was time to go or we would get stuck for hours. The Mayor's wife and my assistant were already in the car waiting, so I got the Mayor back in the car and navigated through the roaring crowd. I looked back at the Mayor. His wife was holding his hand, telling him that he did a good job. In reality, he had taken another step backward for his city.

CHAPTER 13

DO THE RIGHT THING

August 21, 2014 just wasn't the day for the Mayor, seeing that earlier that same day, he had pained the black community again during an interview with CNN anchor Chris Cuomo, in which he referred to Michael Brown's body lying in the street as "it" rather than "he." The poor choice of words displayed the Mayor's insensitivity towards Brown's remains that made it damn near impossible to see any reconciliation. The Mayor didn't have a simple Freudian slip at the podium—his use of the term "it" instead of "he" signaled some real issues with how he viewed black humanity. Even more importantly, the whole world listened to him as he revealed this fact about himself. His choice of words painted a picture of Brown as if he weren't even human. This left a painful scar, not only on the black community at large, but on my heart – I was tasked with helping this man on the murky path of race relations. My task wasn't easy, and his comments made it even harder to keep going.

From the first day I set foot in Ferguson's City Hall, I had pleaded with Mayor Knowles to make a public apology to the family of Michael Brown, and to the black community in the City of Ferguson. I told him, "It's what's best for the city and the black community. You've got to do the right thing."

I believe that, somewhere deep down, Mayor Knowles had a true desire to serve *some* of the black people in Ferguson. He was also very stubborn and full of pride and incredibly ignorant of what the request of the black community in his city actually was.

He didn't understand that he was sitting idly, while the black community suffered. He didn't get that every time he spoke, it was like another stab to the black community's back. I don't even think he realized that he represented a black city, and that *all* black people should be considered, not just the two that he knew.

He didn't want to apologize because he didn't feel like he was connected to Brown's death, and he didn't want to admit responsibility in any form. To him, admitting accountability would be admitting defeat, and admitting defeat would be showing weakness. I think that the Mayor could be capable of making better decisions, but he consistently appeased the wrong people. He had a particular goal in mind, and appeased the right crowd to get it done. Everything else was secondary, even the needs of his residents. I believe part of him wanted to do right, but he also wanted to keep the approval from his core base of staunch Republicans because they'd hinted at the idea of him taking a larger seat, possibly at the state or congressional level.

I had had enough of the interviews. I was sick of him, or anyone else, making matters worse than it already was each time they stepped in front of a camera.

Amazingly, both Mayor Knowles and Chief Jackson asserted that they were looking to change their ways and hear the people. My goal was to get them out and into the black community eventually, but not in front of more cameras or journalists. I wanted them in front of the truly angry people for whom they had no frame of reference. I wanted them to gain cultural competence and equity insight through training in the field with real people and problems, not biased scenarios developed in a classroom setting.

This left the possibility that the Chief and Mayor might be physically or emotionally ruffled, and they might be yelled at, but they had to face the people. I understood that it is easy to take advantage of, or overlook the concerns of, people you don't connect with, and in this instance, a humanizing element was definitely missing between my clients and the public. For example, we all say that we are against child abuse, but we still go and buy products in stores every day that economically empower child trafficking and various abuses. We keep buying because we cannot connect to the pain we are causing. My experience has shown that some people can change when they are enlightened with that new information.

I wanted them to have a front-row seat, looking at the pain in the black community. No matter how much cultural sensitivity training they received, they still didn't fully humanize the impact their efforts left on black people. There was no way we could simulate it so they could receive it.

CHANGE IN OPPRESSOR'S ATTITUDE. *"The oppressor truly helps the oppressed only when he stops viewing them as an abstract category and sees them as unique persons who have been unjustly dealt with, deprived, and cheated. This requires an end to pious, individualistic gestures and risking an act of love. To affirm that people 'should be free, and yet to do nothing tangible to make this affirmation a reality, is a farce'."*

-Paulo Freire

THROWN INTO THE LION'S PIT

NPR and St. Louis Public Radio were set to host an event called "A Panel of Local Community Leaders." Michel Martin, a tenured African-American journalist, was set to host the event. The event was intended to spark a conversation about progress in the community, and encourage open forum from all sides of the table. Invited were Daniel Isom, a retired St. Louis Metropolitan Police Department Chief, Rita Days, a former Democratic State Senator and director of the St. Louis County Election Board, and Reverend Willis Johnson, the pastor of Wellspring Church, where the event was hosted.

Then, there was Mayor Knowles. He had been invited, but most people didn't expect he would attend, given his recent blunders in the national media. I was a bit hesitant too, but again, I thought it would be good for him to be up close and personal with "those people," as the Mayor commonly referred to protestors and others (I had to coach him not to use that phrase).

We showed up early for soundcheck and other security preparations. I stuck with Mayor Knowles and started coaching him, just like I had in the car before Anderson Cooper. He kept assuring me that he was completely fine, and that's what worried me the most. He was under the perception that local public radio would be a "friendly," how PR reps sometimes refer to allies in the media. Seasoned professionals understand that in a crisis situation, the media is not your friend.

"James," I said, "this is no time to mess around. This audience is going to batter you to the ground. If you try to defend yourself, they're going to batter you more. They don't want to hear your excuses. They won't be moved by any of that shit. They're angry, and they're going to stay angry until you guys get it. The best you can do tonight is just take it all in."

I could tell he got a little more heated after I said that. I understood why. I was essentially telling him that I was throwing him into a pit of lions. But that's exactly what had to happen. After a little while, he realized that I was right.

Slowly, the church started filling up. The air conditioning had malfunctioned, so it was hot and sticky. Throw in a few hundred people—angry, hostile people—and the place quite literally felt like an oven on broil. Many people were peeling down as far as they could go. Everyone opened the nearest windows. Then a few people, including the mayor, switched into T-shirts that read, "I AM WELL."

The panelists took their seats, and finally, we got Mayor Knowles on stage. The crowd roared and jeered, but at long last I knew that the Mayor was about to get a concentrated dose of the feelings that had been felt on the outside of these walls for the past three weeks.

There were minutes of unrest before anyone was able to speak.

The night started with an open forum between the panelists. Reverend Johnson expressed that he was hoping that, despite the anger in the community, this event could be used as the first stepping-stone on the path toward success. The crowd cheered on Johnson, an African-American man (though plenty of people were still stirring).

The floor was then opened up, and people from the community were invited to the stage. One after another, men and women both white and black came to the front to express their disgust for the Mayor.

"You are no leader. You do not hear us," one community member said.

Another community member jeered at the Mayor, telling him that the community wants him gone, and asking for his resignation.

To the Mayor's credit, he was a lot less defensive than he had been in the past; however, he still made it clear that he was not going to step down from his position. The highlight of the night was when a young African-American gentleman stood up on the stage in front of the Mayor and asked him if he took any responsibility for the brutality that the police had shown in the streets. When Mayor Knowles denied responsibility, the young man pulled up his shirt to reveal scabs he had sustained from one of the protests. He asserted that the Mayor's police force did that to him with their rubber bullets, and they had harmed his friends with tear gas. The young man demanded that the Mayor apologize. Again, Knowles stood his ground. This time it was the wrong move entirely.

The crowd shouted louder, and I shook my head, while standing at the side of the stage.

Near the end of the event, we received word that police officers were checking license plates in the parking lot to see if there were expired tags. They were looking to arrest anyone they possibly could, and remove them from the event.

I tried to tell the Chief what was happening, but he told me that he was unaware of it. But before he could turn his men down, a speaker on behalf of the church made the announcement to the audience, increasing their anger.

Michel Martin stepped in before too long, and announced the end of the event. I quickly rushed to the stage, said my goodbyes to Senator Days, gave her a hug, and then took off to escort the Mayor towards the back entrance. The crowd began rushing the stage to get face time with the Mayor. When we tried to leave through the back door, we were met with more guests and protesters. They literally had us surrounded, and the crowd inside the building was ramping up quickly. We got through the large group and made it to a back entrance when two females, one with a microphone and recording device and the other a concerned mom and vocal community member, backed the Mayor into a corner.

I let them go at the Mayor for about a good ten minutes before I interrupted. We had our security, mostly undercover and off duty cops, stave off the angry protesters while more backup arrived, and eventually, we were able to take off.

In the car ride back to City Hall, Mayor Knowles was kicking himself.

"I screwed it up again," he said.

I felt like he carried himself a lot better than any previous nights. Was he defensive? Yes. Did he finally make his long awaited apology to the community? No. So maybe there wasn't a ton of headway made with the media, but the one thing that gave me hope for him was that he truly listened.

"Don't sweat it," I said, "You did your best."

Back at City Hall, we parted ways and went home. When I got home I sent him a text message reaffirming my feelings:

Just getting home. Don't beat yourself up, champ. I believe in you, I wouldn't do this project if I didn't. I don't know your religious beliefs but I believe God put us all here for a reason. We were chosen to deal with this. Now we have to listen and learn from the people and respond. Goodnight.

He texted back:

I appreciate it, I will be fine. Just a little war weary. I always believed in leading a purpose driven life, so if this is my purpose, so be it! I just want to succeed. I have never quit, I won't start now.

I had to hand it to him. For all the crap he was going through (and all the stupid decisions he had made), he was still looking toward a positive outcome. I knew he had listened to the people this time. I just hoped that eventually we would convince him to take the next step. I hoped that it sunk in this time.

Unfortunately, I was wrong.

STUBBORN MEETS INCOMPETENT

Sometime after the church meeting, I learned that the Mayor was intent on doing anything *but* apologize to the community. I pursued him every chance I got. Ferguson City Hall is not a huge building, so we couldn't really avoid each other if we tried when he was there.

That's why it was that much crazier when he started ignoring me. True, the Mayor only makes about $300 bucks a month, and is a part-time mayor who works full-time at the license office. But before I started to try to get him to see the error in his ways, he was in City Hall all day.

The media, protestors and the general public were still calling for the Mayor's head in the wake of the NPR event. Ashley Yates was quoted on Twitter after the event, saying:

> We can't talk about how to heal if you (#Ferguson Mayor) won't acknowledge the hurt?

Others replied, "That's why he needs to go!" and "Get him out of office now!" The hashtag *#RecallKnowles* began trending.

I couldn't get through to him. No one could. I didn't see any way that I would anytime soon, so I decided to take matters into my own hands.

The restrictions that the Partnership had placed on us contractors regarding internal e-mails were still in effect. Words like "Michael Brown," "Ferguson," and "Mayor Knowles" were still off-limits, all because they could be easily searched for in public records. The partnership didn't want any of our e-mails to go on public record, because they didn't want us exposing what was going on within the confines of City Hall. Once an e-mail was sent, it was automatically saved as public record.

I decided to turn this rule around and use it for the people's advantage. I started using disallowed keywords left and right. It was my hope that in doing this I could get *someone,* either inside or outside of Ferguson, to see what I was doing and freak out about it. I'm no Eric Snowden, but I had seen enough to make me leave some crumbs for people like Jason Leopold from Vice and Sharon Reed from KMOV. I hoped that they could get the right people to ask some questions. Maybe it would reach the media. Either way, the Mayor's lack of an apology needed attention.

I drafted the following e-mail:

> *As everyone knows there is no way we can begin to heal this situation and change the dialogue without James (Mayor) taking some accountability as a leader.*
>
> *This is my first draft and just reflects what I think should be said. What I hope you and I can do within the next few hours is clean this up so that Stephanie can review with the other attorneys quickly tomorrow to make sure that we eliminate liability.*

I chose to say "eliminate liability" because every written or spoken statement that was not an impromptu personal response by an individual city official, had to go through legal review before going out to the public. City Attorney Stephanie Karr and the other members of the legal team needed to look it over to make sure that the statements would not bring any unwanted liabilities to the city. This was standard protocol.

I continued:

> *I know it's late but we have a short window here as there have been more things happening over the weekend and the city has to make some bold steps this week. My thoughts are that Monday morning we setup a live reading, not traditional press conference where he is open to random questions; followed immediately by exclusive interviews with 1. TV outlet, Radio station, Print outlet (one general market and one African-American focus), and one blogger (all friendlies).*

I said "friendlies" because of what they had been through in their previous interviews. The journalists that they worked with presented themselves to them as though they were doing a positive story. But that was just to get the Mayor to agree to the interview. It seemed like every time Denise would tell the Mayor "friendly" he would put two thumbs up and run towards the set. Once the show producers got him on board, the reporters turned into interrogators.

My e-mail included a document that my copywriter and I had drafted. We needed the Mayor to sign off on it, but we also knew that he would reject it just like he had every other time we had requested an apology. So, we made it a little more hostile than necessary, in hopes that he would reject it, send it back, and we could revise it and make it real and accurate.

I knew there was work to be done, but I wanted to see what the others at City Hall and Common Ground had to say. After a few minutes, each of them had chimed in, and we kept on revising the statement. Amazingly, nobody questioned whether or not it was the right call. In fact, no one questioned whether or not the Mayor was on board.

After a few exchanges and edits, I got an e-mail from Peggy Killian, one of the team members at Common Ground, with one more edit attached including statements about the police force. She wrote:

> *Devin -- Not to complicate things but below is an alternate version of the statement which attempts to meld the two previous statements. Also, following this statement are questions/concerns regarding the statement in general.*
>
> *What do we hope to achieve by doing this?*

Key messages we want to convey -- apology, request for support? To this point, I think the Mayor should avoid asking for the chance to "lead" -- I'm afraid that his motivation for making this statement could be misconstrued if he does that -- i.e. he's apologizing in the hope of not being removed from office (in light of the recall movement underway.)

Who is the primary audience for this statement -- Ferguson residents; St. Louis region; nation?

Finally, I don't think he can say anything about the police, correct? It just seems like that's what's people are most interested in -- police Chief, misconduct of police officers, etc. I fear that talking about change will ring hollow if nothing is done about the police.

After weeks of trying to get an apology from the Mayor, weeks of the black community in Ferguson and the country asking for the same thing, it seemed that Common Ground still didn't get what it was all about either. They didn't understand the humanizing factor of apologizing. Not only had a life been taken, it had been taken by a public servant; hired by the city. Brown should not have been killed. Point. Blank. Period. It doesn't matter if he robbed a store. He didn't receive due process of law. Darren Wilson became both judge and jury, ultimately sentencing Brown to death. Common Ground didn't even understand the political side of things. Mayor Knowles was not under threat of a recall. The time for a recall had passed. I considered not even responding. I was pissed at their lack of organization. But my pen got the best of me. I wrote a quick reply:

The main objective of this apology is to begin the repair of the Mayors Reputation and to address the criticism that he is "tone deaf", "out of touch", "cocky and arrogant" and that he doesn't understand the pain this entire incident and his comments and for that matter his "matter of fact attitude" has caused not only the Black community of Ferguson but around the world. Along with their list of demands the main thing people have asked for is some sense of empathy that he has failed to express.

The primary audience is as follows:

1. *Brown Family*
2. *Ferguson residents in general*
3. *African American Residents (largest population in Ferguson)*
4. *African American community in general (around the world)*

In reference to the comment about police, misconduct of police officers, etc., I wrote:

I think you introduced this as it was not part of my initial apology statement and I agree we should not go there.

After sending off this e-mail, my number one concern became getting Common Ground out of the e-mail thread and away from the handling of any kind of communications. At this point, anyone who was unsure of the apology's intended audience was extremely insensitive to the situation, and therefore did not deserve to contribute. Around noon of that same day, I shot off an e-mail to the city administrators without Common Ground included:

John, Megan, Stephanie,

I have removed Denise and Peggy from this version/conversation because I feel as though they are missing the overall purpose of what we are trying to do and we had already been on the same page so I didn't want to lose momentum. I initially consulted them because myself and other members of the PR team just wanted their perspective as local "PR experts" and to help with possible local appeal for language, etc.

Truth be told, had they advised your team and the Mayor properly from the beginning we would be leaps and bounds ahead of where we are today. So while I understand their desire to be brief, to reduce the specific apology and offer "broad and general strokes", we all have to acknowledge that is exactly what got us here in the first place.

Not being specific about the acknowledgement of the pain, the effects and not addressing audience groups in particular has amplified the rhetoric about how "out of touch" the Mayor is. There is not one Ferguson so we need him and the City council and others to understand this.

Another point is this: Unfortunately, I am the only African American on this team and involved in the messaging process. I have tried to make sure that everyone else understands the nature of the beast we are up against and I wish I had another local African American I could share this with as a sounding board but I can't. Just so you know, if I shared this with even some of the most trusted blacks in the community they would share this and undermine the entire effort. The hurt and pain is very real, people are really mad and conversations about this have to be so close to the vest it is tough to vet but I hope you understand I would not lead you, the Mayor or the City down the wrong path and there is nothing to lose at this point by making this gesture.

We are already at the bottom and need this to at least make room for the bounce back.

Stephanie, the City Attorney, replied a few minutes later:

For what it is worth, I am still supportive of the version 1 that came out this morning. I personally spoke to Peter Dunne last night (he is the attorney who has been appointed by the insurance trust to represent the City in these matters). Devin included our edits in the version 1 that was sent around today. Both Peter and I are comfortable with version 1 as it was sent around earlier. I think that re-doing it or adding or taking away too much from the message as originally prepared and edited makes it unnecessarily complicated at this point.

We sent off the document to the Mayor, and I finally got a hold of him via text message. I said:

Hey just FYI I sent you a statement that was a final from our end having crossed all the Ts and dotted all the I's from a legal perspective. What you should be doing is providing edits that you see fit so we can wrap this up unless you're opposed to the idea in general. Let me know we have a short window on media planning to schedule announcement.

All we could do from there was sit back and wait for the mayor to reply.

He never did.

CHAPTER 14

CALLING OUT THE MAYOR

BEFORE YOU READ ABOUT my issues with the Mayor I wanted to provide a little context on the concept of *white fragility* that may help explain why it's so hard to get white people to understand racism.

> *For white people, their identities rest on the idea of racism as about good or bad people, about moral or immoral singular acts, and if we're good, moral people we can't be racist — we don't engage in those acts. This is one of the most effective adaptations of racism over time—that we can think of racism as only something that individuals either are or are not "doing."*
>
> *In large part, white fragility—the defensiveness, the fear of conflict—is rooted in this good/bad binary. If you call someone out, they think to themselves, "What you just said was that I*

am a bad person, and that is intolerable to me." It's a deep chal-
lenge to the core of our identity as good, moral people.

-Robin DiAngelo

FERGUSON'S SPOKESPERSON

Time and time again, I had encouraged Mayor Knowles to
take a hiatus from speaking out in public. Every time I
turned around, he was igniting the black community and
causing more tension. At the same time, he was becoming
more difficult to deal with. He was frustrated at being the
target of every media attack. I told him it would take time to
recover, and that it wouldn't be easy.

In his mind, he was being treated unfairly. He didn't believe that he deserved all the attacks. But to me, when you
hold certain positions, you have to be accountable for the
grievances of the community at large. That includes what
happens to black residents too. It's not a matter of whether
you did something wrong or not.

He wanted me to help him fight back in the media. I told
him, "Think about the relationship you have with the community like the relationship you have with your wife. If
something is wrong at home and she thinks you did it, and
she's been harboring frustration for other things that have
built up over time, it doesn't matter if you're right or wrong,
you cannot start over until you say I'm sorry. It's like Relationship 101. Until your wife feels that you care sincerely,
you cannot talk about anything. So until you can say something to this city that isn't self-serving, just keep your mouth
shut. If I don't clear it, you don't say it."

He responded, "Oh, so I guess I'm answering to you
now?"

I said, "No, James, you don't, but here are the facts. Someone needs to have a communications plan. You don't have one. Common Ground has a shitty one. I'm the only person in this city who knows how to talk to people in a way that doesn't either insult them or embarrass us. So this isn't about me being in control; it's about taking the time to let the community heal, while you look in the mirror and work on yourself. Because the community is not the problem, it's the system and your failure to see the problems within in it."

"Look," I said. "We can put together a plan in a way that you can be part of the change. Otherwise, it will be an abrupt change. It's up to you. But if you want to be a part of it, it starts with you apologizing to the city."

The mayor replied, "Devin, I've told you, I'm not going to apologize. I'm going to stand my ground. I didn't do anything wrong, so I'm not going to take the blame for someone else who messed up."

He still wasn't getting it. It wasn't about his doing anything wrong. Nobody accused him of pulling a trigger. But the public did see him as someone in a leadership position, which means he should have had more accountability.

I told him, "If someone in a large company screws over millions of people, who's the one that apologizes? It's not the guy who messed up; it's the guy at the top, the company's spokesman. That's because he represents the company as a whole. You're the spokesman of Ferguson, so you've got to represent it. Why is that so fucking hard for you to understand?"

Sometimes people hold a core belief that is very strong. When they are presented with evidence that works against that belief, the new evidence cannot be accepted. It would create a feeling that is extremely uncomfortable, called cognitive disso-

nance. And because it is so important to protect the core belief, they will rationalize, ignore and even deny anything that doesn't fit in with the core belief.

--Frantz Fanon

I never came into Ferguson to save anyone's ass. I came in to make change. And sometimes change means getting rid of someone's ass when they become a liability to the end goal.

THE FINAL STRAW

When you go through a crisis with someone, regardless of what you think of each other, it tends to be a bonding experience. Throughout my first month in Ferguson, the Mayor and I went through a lot, and it felt like we were on completely different pages a lot of the time. He went behind my back numerous times and booked his own interviews; he even tried writing his own talking points--something that no politician in his right mind would do.

For the most part, PR firms and the media work together, so when the Mayor started doing his own thing, it made the partnership look bad. Common Ground and the partnership were working together, but Common Ground owner Denise Bentele was all about herself. Since the partnership was only one of her clients and Katy was just like a buddy, Denise needed to exit the scene so that the media could be attributed to me and my firm, to make us look bad, which contributed to a lot of the bad publicity we would receive later on. Nothing done was an accident or evolved organically.

On September 7, we sent the Mayor his apology statement for revision and approval. I also sent him a text message letting him know what his role was in relation to the statement. He told me he'd get back to me. A good start, I thought. It was the first time he had even acknowledged me in nearly a week.

By September 8, we still had not received any word from Mayor Knowles regarding the apology statement we had sent. He told us he would get back to us, but he never did.

Meanwhile, I had given Common Ground the cold shoulder, which meant my team and I were now handling all of the media communications for the city. I told everyone in City Hall that we were on a media blackout.

"Do not talk to anyone outside of these walls," I said. "Anything you have to say must go through me."

Instead of Common Ground writing up the press releases and sending straight to the media to book interviews, we set it up so my team would start writing them, and then send them to me, John Shaw, and the City Clerk for approval.

That day, I wrote up a press release to send to the news outlets. I did everything but sign my own name, and then I e-mailed it to the administrators for their approval.

That day, the *St. Louis Post-Dispatch* ran an article featuring Ferguson, and for the first time in over a month, it was good publicity. The article highlighted how the Mayor, Chief, and City Council had made some changes in several municipal laws. One of them limited the revenue that could be generated by the court, emphasizing that they wanted punishments to benefit the community, not just the pockets of the courthouse. These were all initiatives that I drew up in order to change the way of thinking inside Ferguson. I wanted to make it so the African-American community could become involved if they chose to (it would ultimately be up to them to participate). I wanted to create a mutually benefi-cial system, so they would be heard instead of marginalized.

But then the Mayor confronted me in an e-mail:

So after busting my fucking ass for this City for 5 weeks, the first positive things that come out of this is attributed to Mark Byrne and our shitty ass judge. I am so fucking pissed right now I can barely contain it. This is fucked up and I am tired of being thrown to the wolves and not given any fucking support. My phone and e-mail was blown up all day by media, and I forwarded on like a good soldier, and I stuck to the media black-out "plan". In the end, they post pictures of me looking distraught and talk about mark and the judge are fixing our problems. From now on, I will talk to whatever fucking media I want, period.

So he effectively went off on me for something that was shedding *positive* light on the city, all because he wasn't high-lighted in the article. I had kept telling him to have patience, but by then, I knew my patience for him had run out. I read the e-mail with my assistant who was sitting next to me. She, along with everyone in City Hall, was well aware of the boil-ing blood between the Mayor and me.

"How the hell are we going to get through to him?" she said.

"We can't," I said, "He's being stubborn...what a jackass. If he knew what was good for him he would keep his mouth shut."

"I'm sick of his bullshit too. If he's not going to be a team player, he can't expect us to keep working with him," my as-sistant stated.

She was right. I pondered the e-mail for a few minutes. I gave myself time to cool off. But by the end of it, I knew I had to take a different approach. I quickly drafted up a response, then let my assistant read it.

"What do you think?" I said. The e-mail was inflammatory, to say the least. But most of all, it had a few bombshells that I knew he wasn't expecting.

"Fuck it," she said, "Send it out."

I clicked send, with copies going to each one of the administrators, and Katy Jamboretz, the contract administrator for the St. Louis Economic Development Partnership. It said:

James,

As a result of the lack of cohesiveness, rampant egos, lack of leadership, and unwillingness to collaborate for the development of a communications and community outreach initiative that will actually benefit "all" of Ferguson and not just the community you live in -- I am out. I sent the press release to everyone including you James and no one filled in their name for the quotes I wrote. Not you, not Mark, no one. Megan and I at the request of the council put marks name in. But now you're worried about who gets the credit? I told everyone to keep their mouths shut, for no one to do interviews because you all just want to talk and even when you don't have shit to say. That's not strategic that's rambling. None of you have a plan on how to move this forward and you don't respect the person who does. None of you respect my experience or what I'm trying to do for you and your community.

Today, you chose to play golf rather than strategize with us about a statement you could have made that would have trumped all of this because you're not the team player I thought you were. I specialize in "communications that benefit people" and you are just trying to benefit yourself.

You are tone deaf, blind and I think you should resign and turn over this seat to someone who really gives a fuck.

He responded promptly:

Devin-

I've stood by you from day one, and have continued to while you've been criticized. To throw out that I took three and half hours (didn't have time for a whole round, and that includes drive time) off to play golf with a couple Ferguson business owners between my DOJ meeting and neighborhood association meetings tonight is petty. I offered to cancel that last night to do whatever you want, and YOU told me to get out and golf, that I needed that. God forbid I would have spent those couple hours at my actual job instead, would I still not be a team player?

I have swallowed a lot of pride and trusted in following your plan, short of apologizing for things I didn't have any hand in, which you wanted me to do. I cannot say I haven't been without flaw, but for you to suggest I haven't played ball is ludicrous.

I gave my input today, even from the golf course, and contrary to your angry words, I have no ego left. But you can't blame me for being tired of being the City, county, and country's whipping boy and not getting the tools to fight back, because I've given too much to this community, the WHOLE community, to still be demonized. It's damn hard to be smeared nonstop and told to be patient. I haven't been looking to benefit myself like dozens of other media hounds running about, I've been patient, though it's frustrating.

I have truly enjoyed working with you, and I feel I've learned a lot from your experiences. I won't even dignify your final angry lashing out with a response, because even in knowing me only a few weeks, you know better.

I went to the Natta Room to gather up my things and move out of the office. I was already mentally checked out. I had been neglecting my family, and I hadn't been taking care of myself physically or emotionally. I was taking on all the stress of the world regarding Ferguson, and I was tired of witnessing the negligence of Old Ferguson, and the mistreatment of New Ferguson. And it was all pointing back to the ignorance within leadership from the partnership, the Governor, the Mayor and the County Executive.

I bumped into the Mayor in the hallway.

"What are you doing?" he asked.

"Getting the fuck out of here," I said.

"You were serious?"

"I'm getting on a plane. I can't deal with this bullshit anymore."

"Devin, we need you guys here. Yes, I was angry, but I was in a tough spot. You know as well as anyone I've dealt with nothing but stress for a month straight. But you got to stick around and see this plan through."

I hesitated.

He said, "You do want to help, right?"

"Yeah," I said, "but ya'll aren't *letting* me help. I can't keep working like this, so if you want me and my team around, we got to do what's best for the community."

"You got it."

"You've said that before."

"Devin, I'm a politician. I need to talk. But I'll listen to you too. We'll do what you say. And we'll have more discretion moving forward. Again, we need you. We're going to fall apart if you leave now."

"Then let's get working," I said.

CHAPTER 15

CITY COUNCIL MEETINGS

IN THE MONTH FOLLOWING Michael Brown's death, I served as the social link between the most consistent protest group leaders and the administrators in City Hall. My team and I were still working around the clock. I would attend roll calls at the beginning of every police shift, and establish the communication channels for any incidents or reports that might or might not have turned into a news story. That would entail identifying who would get me the details, the spokesperson, and going over the dos and don'ts. Our team would split up so there was always someone with the Chief, and someone at City Hall.

In the evening, we would attend community events and interviews with the Mayor, Chief, or council. Then at night, we would meet back at City Hall and go over strategies with the Chief. The majority of the activities, especially regarding riots or other forms of civil disobedience, started late at night. The only people who respond to this sort of action, at this time of night, are police officers. Our purpose of staying with the Chief was to monitor this activity, so that we would be the first to know what happened. We couldn't depend on the police department to give us accurate information, so we decided to monitor the activity ourselves.

In the afterhours of the night, we were out in the community. We worked with one protest group's leadership to help them establish more organized protesting plans. That way, they could encourage peaceful protesting to avoid getting arrested for sport. We also explained why certain tactics would only create more tension. Many prominent black "leaders" would actually lead protesters into harm's way, even when they had been given intel that law enforcement was on high alert. Some politicians went and got arrested on purpose, advising others to follow, knowing that the large demonstrations and large scale acts of civil disobedience would only increase government spending on law enforcement for things like more weapons, more equipment, more vehicles, more training, etc. To me, none of this made any sense, if the objective was really to change the fact that government was this large oppressive entity. It's counter-intuitive to invite a stronger military presence when you know the real danger associated with the way military sees drug and crime areas. To me, it was clear that we needed a document, a plan, and people working together to accomplish it.

I was working constantly, with every department of government and nearly every community group in Ferguson.

Many times, I didn't sleep at all. I just kept working through the night, and started all over again with the Chief in the morning.

Many people told me that I was the only thread of hope that they had. I explained to them how I had been working hard with the Mayor, and while I didn't call him out as an idiot to anyone publicly, I explained that it had been hard getting him to understand what the people in the black community were going through.

In early September, I got my first taste of social media backlash, when an infographic started circulating amongst protest groups on Instagram and Twitter. It showed my picture next to the Mayor's, and the caption under my picture read:

> *Ferguson has hired him to get you to go away. If you talk to him, you're stabbing yourself in the back. He does not support your rights. He does not support your cause.*

A friend had forwarded the image to me while I was actually out in the streets. When I saw it, I knew what was coming next and started to prepare for it.

It's all too common in the social media age for news stories and "truth" to spread among people who have no idea what they're talking about. It's easy to make the rounds when you have a sensationalized headline, and a well-known enemy like Mayor Knowles. The fact is, the black community was angry. I had said so time and time again. I knew first hand because I had been immersed in it, and I was the only one trying to work with the city to better engage the black community.

When I attended demonstrations, some protesters would start yelling at me, saying, "You're one of them!" If they approached me angrily, I would listen and let them vent. I didn't get scared. I didn't feel threatened. Was it difficult to have random people shouting at me in public out of nowhere? Yes, but, at the same time, I knew that their anger was not for me, it was for the city and the Mayor; it was from the hurt and pain from all the abuse under Charlie Dooley's watch; it was all the broken promises of the politicians. Once they finished speaking, I would acknowledge their steaming frustration, bottled-up anger and pain. Then I would calmly explain why I was there, and what I was really doing. I would tell each one of them short stories about my background to show them that I knew exactly how they felt. They interrupted me multiple times. I remained calm. I stuck it out. Most importantly, I shared why I felt like God gave me a second chance. Once they saw that I was really working for the best of our community, and not "for the system," the tension faded. By the end of the conversation, we would be smiling and hugging and talking about hobbies.

It is important to note that although I did receive harsh treatment from some people, the members of the protest groups I worked with never turned on me. Most of the harsh treatment came from people who didn't know me or who were hearing of me, or meeting me for the first time. My approach was grassroots-based and one-on-one, because I believe that one must leave his/her office and start over at that point. I wasn't interested in giving Ferguson a marketing campaign, I wasn't introducing a #HealSTL movement, and I wasn't talking about jobs or job fairs. I aimed to speak to the humanity of the situation. My community engagement plan was about personal interactions. I wanted to, and still want to, create an environment where people routinely know the officers' names and where they live. Officers know the same of the civilians, but there is no working power dynamic between the two groups. This may be a long shot, but it is a strong model for change in America. My experience providing strategic planning and marketing communications services to the government and corporations for nearly ten years should warrant someone listening to what I have to say.

When I hear opposition of my plan, I think of Albert Einstein and the many times that he failed before he succeeded. I know that now. The government sets the standards for our living conditions as black people. I want to change that, no matter how far-fetched the vision sounds today. The people working with me in Ferguson gave me the encouragement needed to keep going with my vision and to keep focused on my plan. I definitely wasn't the man that some protestors were trying to make me out to be. I knew that the protestors were only going to get more vocal, and I couldn't blame them. I was one of them, too.

SHUT IT DOWN

The city was scheduled to hold its first public council meeting since the death of Michael Brown. We had already had plenty of council meetings beforehand, but they were always behind closed doors. This one was big. In fact, it was so big that we had to reschedule the meeting multiple times because we couldn't accommodate all the people who were planning on attending.

We finally set the date for September 9, and moved the event to Greater Grace Church. After announcing the event, media trucks were parked in the Greater Grace parking lot for days leading up. The pastor just about used a few words that weren't welcome on church grounds. He was furious that the media was taking over what was supposed to be a sacred place. The media were also intruding on his congregation, even going so far as to stake out and attempt to draw interviews from people entering and leaving the building. The media was truly disrespectful to his property, and it nearly caused us to have to pull the plug.

That evening, there was a slight drizzle and the weathermen had reported showers; most of the Ferguson city officials were hoping that the rain would reduce the crowd attendance. The Chief had implemented high security measures and would advise me of any changes in status, I would then advise all of the community leaders about the new developments. Much like when a celebrity or politician makes an appearance, they had to establish emergency escape routes in case the crowd bombarded us. We had also received multiple death threats to the Chief, Mayor, and others, so we had to establish checkpoints for media personnel and examine all of their equipment to make sure they weren't pointing anything other than cameras at the people on stage.

The media attention made the NPR event from a few weeks earlier seem like a preamble. This was showtime.

Less than an hour before the doors were set to open, however, some dark clouds started rolling into Ferguson. Before long, it started raining, and people started running to get into the entranceway. Still, plenty of people stood drenched in the rain, waiting. Nothing was going to stop them from getting into that building.

Behind the church's stage, my crew had our media room set up and was watching, as media crews checked in, and church volunteers were pulling together furniture to assemble the panel where the council members would sit. It was anything but a conventional council meeting.

Behind the stage in a separate room, it looked like they were preparing for a trial. Every single one of them was nervous. I walked past John Shaw and a few other council members, who were going over their notes.

"Where's Knowles?" I said.

John looked up, and motioned to the restroom.

I went over to the event coordinator and asked, "Have you been given the green light to let people in?"

She replied, "You need to talk to the Chief."

After only a few minutes, they started letting people in, and the chapel seats were filled all the way to the back. I remembered how we had been bombarded on stage at the previous meeting, and had to get security to help us flee. This time we knew better, and had a decoy escape route to throw people off.

Finally, the mayor came out of the restroom. He took a seat at the couch with the others backstage, and I went to talk to them.

I said, "There's no easy way to say it. This isn't your normal council meeting. You're about to go through hell. You're going to feel the heat, and it might make you want to quit on stage. But this is first time the people have had you all in the same room since the tragedy happened. They're angry, and they need to vent. To you, that may seem like a bad thing, but it's not a bad thing at all. Venting frustration is a part of moving forward. They *need* to scream and yell. So when that happens, don't get defensive. Don't cower. Sit up straight and take it. Be humble. Most of all, listen. The audience needs you to hear them."

They were all bewildered. John took a handkerchief out of his pocket and dabbed the sweat from his face.

I went on, "You need to remember that crowd out there that you so easily refer to as a mob, has many of the people that you represent among them. I know that everyone isn't a Ferguson resident, but what the people feel was done to the black community exceeds the borders of Ferguson. Black folks and social justice advocates all over the world are angry, and they want to be heard. They're going to yell at you. But if you *listen*, it won't be that bad. If worse comes to worst, I'll be right here to advise and we have Bishop Larry Jones to help with crowd control."

The meeting was divided up into two parts. As I mentioned before, the event was a City Council meeting at its core, which meant that business had to be conducted. The first part of the meeting was set aside for the council members to speak to the community and discuss new legislation. The second half was set aside for citizens to speak. They had two microphones set up, one in each aisle, and they would line up in the aisle behind them, taken turns going back and forth, venting their concerns. Anyone who wanted to would get three minutes to address whatever he or she wanted. Since the event was large in both size and scale, people were lining up in droves to speak. These people had waited in the rain for the opportunity to address their concerns. No one was going to let this moment slip by.

A volunteer for the church moderated the crowd and introduced each one of the council members to the audience. As they did, the crowd started booing. It was like they were announcing the starting lineup at a basketball game, and the council was the away team. News crews in the back captured it all in high definition.

Approximately twenty minutes after its scheduled time, the council meeting finally kicked off. Mayor Knowles was the first to speak. He kindly thanked the audience for coming and went on to address the new legislation that we had been working on for weeks. The legislation introduced a set of policies that barred the municipal court from receiving so much revenue from tickets and fines. This was a huge concern among the African-American community--they were targeted by police officers, and felt that the tickets against them were being used to fund the city. In fact, the Department of Justice's report on Ferguson showed that although African-Americans make up 67% of Ferguson's population, 85% of people subject to a vehicle stop were African-American, and 90% who received a traffic ticket were African-American.[11]

The crowd applauded at the new legislation. It was the first time in a month that I had seen the community show any positivity toward the Mayor, and I thought it to be a step in the right direction for him. It showed him that New Ferguson was not just made up of protestors wanting him to be recalled. They were people who understood the legislation and were yearning eagerly for change to actually take place. The audience was obviously applauding the legislation, however, and not the man delivering the message.

The second half of the meeting was reserved for public comment. The audience was so dialed into the agenda that they didn't even let the council members finish their statements before rushing to the microphones placed in the aisles. Within seconds, the atmosphere became hostile once again,

---

[11] The United States Department of Justice: Civil Rights Division, *Investigation of the Ferguson Police Department: Racial Bias.* (March 2015): 4. Web. 25 June 2015.

in the eyes of the city officials. I would say that the atmosphere was appropriate, given the circumstances.

"How are you planning on engaging a community when you don't even know that people are angry at you?" one protester stated. Another protester said, "You said there's no racial divide in Ferguson. There must be two Fergusons, 'cause you're staring at the divide right now."

The crowd roared.

Another man stood up, wearing a black t-shirt with the white letters, I AM MIKE BROWN.

"I'll tell you what," the man said. "You're looking to make peace with this community? You need to put Darren Wilson behind bars. Until that happens, you're going to get riots in the streets. You're going to be fearing for your life."

A young lady took the microphone from him. "You guys don't understand. You act like Mike Brown isn't even a human being. You left him out there in the streets like a dog. Tell me something. You have kids? You tuck them into bed at night? Well, think if they were walking out on the streets and got shot. How would you feel?"

It was a dagger, and it hit hard. One by one, people expressed their utmost concerns and fears for their community. Late into the night, the crowd started chanting, "Shut it down! Shut it down!" They threw up their hands, mirroring the "Hands Up, Don't Shoot" gesture replicated by millions of people around the world. The gesture would quickly materialize into a symbol of non-violent resistance against the police, but that night, the people were mirroring Mike Brown's gesture toward Darren Wilson on that fateful August night.

I felt a vibration in my pocket, and I checked my phone. It was a text message from John Shaw asking me to pull him off the stage when I could. I looked up at him on stage, and he was looking right back, the color gone from his face. Halfway into the meeting, I pulled John off of the stage.

The event went on for three hours. We had to cut it off at ten o'clock, and even then, there were people waiting in lines that went out the back doors of the chapel, hoping to be heard.

Before people left, Mayor Knowles made one more address, announcing the establishment of a civilian review board, which would allow the hiring process in Ferguson to bring in more diversity.

The Civilian Review Board was *exactly* what this city's police force needed, but the truth is that the Mayor had no idea what he was saying. He just used it as a buzzword to try and make it seem like they were actually doing something. In reality, they had nothing, and they didn't know what they were doing.

The announcement of the Civilian Review Board serves as a perfect example of how the city would speak before there was any substance to their words or work. For me, it was a chance to show them, yet again, why Ferguson officials needed to stop talking and start strategizing. Immediately after they announced the Review Board, people in the community, media, and other elected officials began to pull the idea apart. Their main criticism was weak language in the document. This didn't have to happen if the Mayor hadn't disclosed so much information so early. We were planning a review board, and the Mayor was in one of the meetings and copied on some of the e-mails. Although Megan and I were still working on the specifics, city leadership thought it would be good to introduce the idea prematurely.

CHAPTER 16

ESTABLISHING A CIVILIAN REVIEW BOARD

IMMEDIATELY AFTER THE COUNCIL meeting, the city came under scrutiny for announcing the Civilian Review Board. The plan wasn't even fully crafted yet. We had been working on it with the city over the previous couple of days, and every once in a while, the Mayor would sit in on our meetings. He didn't fully understand it, but he liked the sound of it, so they decided to introduce it during the council meeting.

I could no longer trust anyone in the region, so I had to look for outside sources to help us establish a civilian review board. The city had no idea what those words meant, but at the same time, neither did any of the supposed "black leaders." There was so much division, that there was no one that you could get to work together long enough to get past "meaningful dialogue." If you did have a meeting that seemed authentic, shortly after the meeting was over, media was waiting for you outside. A tweet, a comment, or a post followed this on someone's timeline. Everything about it was very tacky.

It just so happened that the National Association for the Civilian Oversight of Law Enforcement (NACOLE) was in Kansas City at the time, getting ready for their annual conference. NACOLE is a non-profit organization geared towards improving police oversight in the United States. They advise law enforcement agencies on complete system overhauls, and focus on creating a dialogue both internally and between law enforcement and the community.

I exchanged a few e-mails with NACOLE's President Brian Buchner. When he saw the word "Ferguson," he was immediately on board. He and his team had been following Ferguson closely. Brian and his family had roots in Missouri, so he felt a strong personal connection every time he turned on the news. He made it clear that he wanted to dedicate his time to helping our efforts.

Brian was deeply passionate about creating a positive bond between policemen and people. He wanted people to know that there were good cops out there, but most of all, he wanted to *create* good cops. He hated reading stories like Michael Brown's, because he knew they only dug the chasm between civilians and law enforcement that much deeper.

He had agreed to bring his whole team on board to do one-on-one training with the city. He invited the city officials to attend the NACOLE conference in Kansas City, so that we could set up a meeting with his team of experts from all over the country, and strategize to strengthen the Review Board.

An Alternate Route

I had been having trouble trying to convince the city that they needed the training and oversight that NACOLE could provide to establish a credible civilian oversight initiative. I told officials that NACOLE was willing to offer their assistance, but they didn't pay it any mind. I couldn't tell if they thought they didn't need the training, or if they were just unwilling to work with me.

I was on the phone with Brian at one point, explaining the stubbornness of the organization to him. Brian thought it over for a moment, and then got up the gall to hit me with a bombshell.

"Devin," he said, as he peered over a public records e-mail, "Do you think Ferguson's leaders are ignoring you because you're young and black?"

I stopped. I had never really thought of it that way. Of course the thought had crossed my mind from time to time in other circumstances because, as a professional black man, you always question whether you are being discriminated against because of your color. In the middle of the crisis, however, it was eye-opening to have a white man in California point out that it might be the color of my skin that was a factor in how they treated me or regarded my advice. But it was a factor everywhere, with everyone. How did I not see it? All this time, I felt like their main issue was that they were lacking the cultural competence to fully understand the issues.

I said, "I have a theory about the racial climate here. Many people here are not racists, but they're incredibly insensitive and incompetent when it comes to cultural and racial issues. Being a racist is intentionally trying to hurt someone. Insensitivity is not knowing any better."

"Either way, it's wrong," he said. I couldn't argue with that.

"So let's try this," he said. "You've been having trouble getting them to listen to you. Let's see if they'll listen to me."

He started drafting a letter--an official NACOLE letter--with the intention of sending it to the administrators. For half an hour, we traded drafts back and forth to make it more appealing. Finally, when we were done, it read as follows:

To the Honorable Mayor Knowles and Distinguished

Members of City Council:

As President of the National Association for Civilian Oversight of Law Enforcement (NACOLE), I write to offer NACOLE's support and assistance as the City of Ferguson works to rebuild the essential relationship between the Ferguson Police Department (FPD) and the community it serves, in part by establishing a citizens' review board to oversee and help improve the FPD's operations

Established in 1995, NACOLE is a 501(c)(3) not-for-profit association of law enforcement oversight agencies and practitioners that works to enhance accountability and transparency in policing and build community trust through civilian oversight. To further our mission, we hold an annual conference that brings together the growing community of ci-vilian oversight practitioners, law enforcement officials, journalists, elected officials, students, community members, and others to meet and exchange information and ideas about issues facing civilian oversight and law enforcement.

In addition to the annual conference, NACOLE publishes a regular newsletter, hosts an e-mail listserv, conducts regional training, offers a professional credential in the practice of over-sight, administers a professional mentoring program for newer oversight practitioners, and provides assistance to communities looking to start or review their existing oversight cess. More information about NACOLE can be found on our website, www.nacole.org.

We understand from recent news reports that Ferguson will be considering the establishment of a citizens review board to oversee the FDP. As the premiere – and only – professional as-sociation of experts in the field of civilian oversight, NACOLE offers its assistance to you and the greater Ferguson communi-ty as you begin this process.

This year's annual conference, our 20th, will be held in Kansas City, Missouri from September 14-18, 2014. I am hopeful that members of the Ferguson government, police department, and community will consider joining us at the conference to take advantage of the only oversight-specific training available in the country, engage in networking opportunities with oversight practitioners and other groups of interested stakeholders from across the country and around the world, and see first-hand the value and intelligence behind establishing and maintaining vi-brant civilian oversight.

Kind regards,

Brian Buchner

President
NACOLE

It turned out Brian was right. Within two minutes, City Manager John Shaw wrote us back:

Yes, we need to do this right away.

A ROAD TRIP

It was very difficult for me to get Ferguson administrators to agree on anything. When I told them that we had a conference to go to, they all made gestures of frustration and sighed, but when I told them it was a road trip to Kansas City, they were all smiles!

That was the one trump card I had. Almost everyone in City Hall had been in Ferguson for the past month. The Mayor had not set foot outside of the greater St. Louis Area. Chief Jackson was about ready to buckle under the pressure, and the administrators were no different. Getting out of town would be like a vacation for them, even if it were just on the other side of the state. The minute I said "hotel suite," they were on board.

I got on a phone with a connection I had in Kansas City at a hotel. I booked rental cars, because every car we rode in seemed to come under attack. People who were angry knew where we all lived, and what cars we would be in (they even knew about the route I took on my bike). We couldn't risk everyone being in the same car at once, so I split us up in groups.

Mayor Knowles kept asking me about the conference, and what to expect. You would have thought he was going to

Paris, because he was so excited to be in another city. It was like culture shock to him.

"What are we expecting from media at this event?" he asked.

"Hopefully nothing," I said.

"Nothing?"

"Yeah, we gotta keep you guys under the radar as much as possible. If word gets out that you're there, you might get bombarded just like you do in Ferguson."

The mayor seemed frustrated. I didn't get it. Just like Common Ground, he was still trigger-happy when it came to media. He was still under the impression that things would be better if he just said as much as he could. He was trying to dig his way out of a hole.

"What about our talking points?" he said.

"What talking points?"

He opened up a folder. "I brought our talking points we made a while back, "he said. "I brought our notes in case we had any interviews."

I hadn't gone over talking points with the Mayor in quite some time because he had gone rogue.

I sighed. "James," I said, "I think you're missing the point here. This isn't a media opportunity. This is a conference where you will be attending seminars and classes so that you can become more engaged in the community. You are not going as a spokesperson or guest participant. You are here to learn, while Brian from NACOLE, John and the Chief can work out the details on next steps."

He was pretty pissed when I said that, but I could tell he knew that I was right. He didn't have anything to gain from talking anymore than he already had. It might even be a bad thing if people knew he was out of town. What if people

turned this story around to make it look like he was fleeing
the city? I wanted to acknowledge the stress he'd had been
through without detracting from the main point. Regardless
of whether the constant attacks against the Ferguson administration were warranted or not, the city officials served as a
scapegoat for a lot of situations they only played a small part
in. As humans, we can't forget to acknowledge the abuse the
administration endured just to reap whatever reward they
received. The threats were bad for everyone, and I know that
both the people on my team and I sought professional help
after the ordeal was over. Dealing with a cocktail of racism,
the media, corporate greed, hate, violence, chaos, bickering
and human suffering is a recipe for mental anguish. I want to
acknowledge the mental strain that everyone, on both sides,
went through. Mayor Knowles, as hardheaded as he was,
needed this trip. I wanted him to enjoy himself.

"Just relax, keep a low profile, try to learn something, and
enjoy the time away," I said.

"I'm planning on enjoying getting away from Hell," he
said.

A few moments passed. The mayor spoke again: "I don't
know what I'm going to do with all those shirts, though."

"What shirts?" I said.

"The shirts in back," he said, and I immediately remembered the big cardboard box he had stuffed into the trunk
before leaving.

"What were you planning to do?"

"I was going to hand them out to people. They say, 'I
LOVE FERGUSON' on them."

I shook my head. "I don't think you're going to find many
people who love Ferguson there. So you should leave those."

KANSAS CITY

I rode over to the conference with John Shaw, the City Manager. He hadn't been out of the county since the death of Brown either, but he was a little more reserved about it than the Mayor. I knew John had been pretty traumatized by everything in Ferguson. We all had been. It was tough to deal with. Our lives and our relationships suffered because we were putting so much time and energy into everything. Now Ferguson was under investigation from the DOJ, which meant that John was under investigation too.

John was on the phone with his wife, and I could tell they were in a pretty heated argument.

"Damn," he said after hanging up, "It's getting to be too much."

"It's fucked up," I said, "there's no denying that." It was the first time since the beginning that he and I had ever been alone one-on-one. I didn't know him much outside of the Natta Room, but the one time we did sit down was when I disclosed my background and he disclosed his. Here in the car, we were able to shed our titles and be straight with each other.

"It's totally fucked up," he said, "I can't focus anymore. I got the DOJ breathing down my back, the Governor's office still won't commit to helping us, and the Mayor's still being a jackass."

I kept driving. I didn't have anything to say to that. We were all in the same boat. John had come under scrutiny lately when he claimed that the money the city was collecting from traffic tickets was a good thing. People saw that as his being racist, since most ticketed individuals were African-American. My experiences with John taught me that he wasn't a racist at all; it was the system that was racist. John embraced diversity, and was an integral part in approving most of the progressive measures during our time in Ferguson. I sympathized with his position and wanted things to get better for him.

We arrived at the conference center, and John kept pretty quiet as we went into the building. I patted him on the back, "You got this," I said.

We all checked into the conference, using code names to keep a low profile.

Throughout the event, people kept staring at us and making comments. People definitely recognized us, so we had to split up. The Mayor was hassled a few times in between seminars, and he was even bombarded by a few angry attendees. But, most people kept their cool after being confronted by conference security. Brian did a good job of making sure we didn't get too much flack.

After a few sessions, we met up with the leadership team from NACOLE and spent some time creating the outline for the Civilian Review Board Needs Assessment, after a few quick introductions. I shared the information I had gathered from the community, detailing what they wanted to see most out of the program, so there could be some authentic framework instead of the usual Ferguson posturing. Everyone from NACOLE immediately recognized that I "got it" and quickly informed the Chief and John that they should listen to me.

Once it was agreed that they would partner, we setup for a photo shoot to capture the image that would go with the announcement we would later craft. The closing comments were from NACOLE's past president and former Chief of Police, who instructed Chief Jackson on what they needed to do to get the board implemented. This meant working in conjunction with Ferguson citizens who were otherwise not involved in the municipal government, so that they could keep checks and balances with the police department, and ensure that they were doing things the right way.

Once we were finished, my team wrote up the press release announcing Ferguson's partnership with NACOLE, and the long-awaited establishment of the Civilian Review Board.

CHAPTER 17

PROTEST AND STREETFEST

WHEN IT CAME TO identifying locations for events and public meetings, I always went to Ferguson's event planner, Toni Roper. Toni was the only African-American I ever saw on the city's payroll who interacted with the community. Her family owned Roper's Ribs, a beloved family restaurant on Florissant Avenue. The Ropers are well-known and respected in both New and Old Ferguson communities.

Many people watching the news at home from around the country don't realize how large Ferguson was geographically. Ferguson is a suburb of St. Louis with a very extensive cityscape. This is important because the Ferguson protests, while many in number, were isolated within a small section of the city. Black people live in a small part of the city, and most of the chaos took place within that area. When we say there is a racial divide, we are not only talking about race, but also the physical and economic separation that comes from the ills of systemic racism. In these environments, it is very possible to have peace on one side of the city, and chaos on the other.

In spite of all the protests, there were still Old Ferguson community activities taking place. For instance, the Ferguson Farmer's Market still took place, which is a long-standing tradition on Saturdays. In fact, if you had Googled Ferguson, Missouri on August 8, 2014, you would have seen a snapshot of people sharing meals and having fun with their families.

On September 14, 2014, however, the unrest made its way to the Farmer's Market. Early in the morning, protesters began pouring through the makeshift alleyways between booths. People were carrying signs and shouting through megaphones. Chief Jackson made an appearance and even managed a peaceful conversation with a circle of young black men.

Many Old Ferguson residents were emotionally shut off from the unrest near West Florissant Avenue. They kept themselves numb to the pain and suffering going on within the black community around them, to the point that they practically denied it was happening.

After several peaceful demonstrations, a different group of protesters returned the following week. This was a paid group, meaning that the people were actually paid to protest. Accordingly, this group was disorderly compared to the paid protesters, who "knew their rights" well. The group kept trying to push the envelope with both market attendees and law enforcement. They were sent there strictly to agitate, and they caused heated confrontations. Some people even dove in front of cars, trying to get hit, just so they could cause a larger disturbance. The people were trained as part of their agreement for payment. They were taught laws that neither the Chief nor the City Attorney knew regarding protesting rules, nor the legal bounds of police officers managing crowds.

When things like this happened, I would have to work harder to help the police differentiate between the real protestors and the actors. For those who think that every police officer meant to hurt people who were just protesting as part of their rights, all I can say is that at times it was very, very hard to tell who was going to just practice civil disobedience from someone who was about to practice taking someone out.

The demonstration appeared disorganized on purpose. It was set up to make the regular protestors look bad and increase tensions between New and Old Ferguson. It worked. Several people were arrested on both sides. It left a sour taste for the market-goers, and shed yet another bad light on both protestors and the Ferguson Police Department.

THE FSBD MEETING

At the next Ferguson Street Business District meeting, the market-goers made their voices heard.

In the Ferguson Street Business District meeting, all of the business owners in the district meet to talk about things going on in the area that impact their businesses. The topics would cover crime, rental housing and real estate, tourism and foot traffic, among other topics. There were dozens of white business owners, but despite a majority black population, there were less than three black business owners ever in the meetings. It was always a white-dominated atmosphere. The evidence of another instance of institutional racism, where cultural incompetence impedes any progress for minority-owned companies.

Due to increased racial tension, we asked Darryck Dean, from the Department of Justice, to facilitate the meeting. We wanted to create a "safe space" for us to talk about race among the business owners without any intimidation, insults or animation. We felt like this would keep the attendees from getting out of hand. The Mayor, the Chief, my team and I were there, and if prior meetings had taught us anything, we knew to at least anticipate some chaos.

During the meeting, the few black business owners in attendance voiced their opinions. The owner of Cathy's Kitchen on South Florissant stood up and said that although his business was taking economic hits and sales were down, the protesters were a part of the community, and they needed to be respected. You could tell that he understood the need for the protest and the pain coming from those screaming.

Many white business owners couldn't sympathize with the people, and thought the protests were unnecessarily damaging their livelihood.

"We can't let these terrorists take over our town!" one angry businessman yelled, his face beet red and his throat quaking. "They took our market, and now they think they can take over the whole damn town! We ain't backing down from this! We ain't giving up our town!"

One gentleman was bold enough to call the people a bunch of homeless, jobless thugs. That hurt me personally, because I had been among both groups, and I knew that they were on the opposite side of the spectrum. The funny thing was, most of the people protesting in the streets were just like them, and the only difference was their color and purpose for coming together.

The protest groups consisted of teachers, mailmen, ministers, students, and neighbors. Some were homeless or jobless, but that represented the minority of people. The man's comment reflected not only his racism and ignorance, but the shared, collective attitudes of many Ferguson residents just like him. Many people at the meeting shared his sentiments. People threatened to bring their dogs out on the protesters, and one even mentioned that he was ready to hose them down.

The meeting was supposed to be a quick briefing, but it turned into a two-hour Q and A session. Near the end, I was finally given a chance to speak.

"Look," I said, "I understand that you feel threatened by the protests. It makes sense. But the truth is that we're not going to be able to do anything about it right now, no matter how hard we try. The best thing we *can* do is to try to understand why the black community and the protest groups are upset. We need to acknowledge people are in pain. Discrediting and disagreeing with them only contributes to the tension."

An older lady stood up and cleared her throat: "I've been in Ferguson all my life. I've watched it grow, and it used to be a *good* town. I'm tired of having these animals take it over. All I have is one question: When are we getting our Ferguson back?!"

The word she had used—*Animals*. I was shocked, appalled, and enraged at the same time. I shook my head. This lady still wasn't getting it. "Ma'am," I said, "You need to check the demographics. Ferguson hasn't been your town for a long time."

My View on the Protest Groups

I spent a lot of time with protest groups, both young and old. I spent a lot of time with gang members, who, despite outside opinion, were equally passionate about seeing peace within the city limits. In fact, many of the gangs of North County were in many ways much more organized than the protest groups and law enforcement. They were structured and had a common goal to protect their neighborhoods and protestors exercising their rights.

The problem stems in part from the fact that St. Louis is a Midwestern city. Despite its geographical proximity to the south, it was never really touched by the civil rights movement of the 1960's. Thus, there was never a large-scale revolution in the city. There were no sit-ins, no marches, nothing. There was never anyone who stood up and pushed for African-American rights. Because of this, the African-American community was inherently suppressed. They had never really riled themselves up and pulled together because there was no catalyst. I like to think that, as of 2014, the black community was finally getting its moment. They just needed to execute properly.

Several protest groups came to me for advice on how to advance from a group of people in the streets to an actual entity with a community-driven mission statement. These groups wanted something bigger, something that could create jobs, teach people their rights, encourage people to vote and make them more sustainable.

The black community needed a figure to stand up and bring cohesiveness to their movement. But no one emerged, because politics and money were more important than change and humanity.

If the African-American community wants to mobilize teams to expand and unite the movement, we need to have leaders with integrity, who want to do the right thing for all people, and last but not least, leaders who see everyone as equally valuable. Not leaders who are posturing for a seat or perks. Equity-focused community building is the key. It's not about advocating for a black takeover that would put blacks who manipulate other blacks into power; it is a real paradigm shift where we get away from using "their" lens to define us.

Protest by itself, from a marketing perspective, is just an outreach tactic. It can be compared to a fundraising event or a parent-teacher conference. It draws attention and makes the cause visible, and the black community needs that. The real movement, however, needs to come from a deeper place, because what actually causes change is understanding the business aspect to protesting. Just as the government plans large-scale projects such as real estate, tourism, and development, the black community will have to have a plan with realistic objectives if we want to achieve sustainability. Our objectives should be based on what we want to accomplish, and should allow us to approach the entire point of our mission through a lens of equity. We had the dream in the 1960's with Martin Luther King; now we need to pick up where his dream left off and create a plan with deliverables that people today can actually accomplish, or none of our efforts will ever change the policies that currently enslave us.

CUE STREETFEST

StreetFest, scheduled for September 26, 2014, is the biggest annual fall festival put on by the city. It includes food booths, vendor booths, craft booths, arts, games, shows, and concerts all wrapped into one. All eyes were on this event, which meant it would be a statement for Ferguson. It would either be a time of recreation, bonding, and healing, or it would be a time of further calamity on a scale much larger than the Ferguson Farmer's Market.

Because my planning was at the community level, I also performed crisis planning around the events in the city to try to reduce the racial tension. While I continued to encourage protest, I didn't want any of the dysfunctional demonstrations that had gone on over the past few weeks. This was because many of the white business owners were also gun owners who had the right to conceal and carry. The racism at this point was very overt, and I was afraid that another black person would be killed because one of the white business owners was scared and fired his or her weapon. This was a very real fear, given the circumstances. If they felt at all threatened by any of the protesters in New Ferguson, they could start a fist fight and kill someone and try to claim self-defense. The racist white people stuck together. Honestly, it reminded me of the Klan. Being from Tennessee, where the KKK was founded, I used to watch Klan meetings at various statues around Memphis in honor of Nathan Bedford Forest, a general in the Confederate Army and a leader in the KKK. As such, my concerns were filled with fear, but I wanted to be on the side of caution to keep peace. I felt that any altercations between races would only further divide the community.

Toni Roper was in charge of promoting the event city-wide. She sent me this e-mail in mid-September:

> Devin,
>
> Could you please review the statement below for the participants in Ferguson's upcoming event.
>
> Thank you,
>
> Toni Roper

Attached was a promotional flyer for StreetFest:

> The 2014 Ferguson StreetFest event will continue as scheduled. We understand your concerns about this year's festivities, due the recent events that have taken place in Ferguson. Over the past couple of weeks, we continued with the Ferguson Farmers Market, Hispanic Festival, Citywalk Concert Series and Food Truck Mondays.
>
> All of these events took place in the vicinity of where StreetFest will take place, without any issues. We did increase security, and will do so during this month's celebration. The violent activities we have all witnessed through the media have taken place late at night and on West Florissant Rd., a few miles away from Victorian Plaza where StreetFest will take place on South Florissant Rd.
>
> We want to assure you that we feel comfortable proceeding with StreetFest. We also feel that continuing with this event will help the community to heal from this unfortunate situation. Refunds will not be granted. Thank you for your participation and we look forward to another successful event.
>
> Sincerely,

The StreetFest Committee

I liked that we had addressed the unrest in the community, but I felt that it came off a little too deficit-focused. This event was meant to bring joy to the community. With many of the city's business owners already reaching for their rifles, we didn't want this to come off as negative. I sent the e-mail off to one of my writers and asked her to come up with some better wording. Then I headed off to a meeting with the Chief to talk about safety measures for the event.

SECURITY MEASURES

There was still a large number of protests going on in Ferguson. Even though they were confined to areas around West Florissant Avenue, it seemed like a war zone every single day in every part of the town. There were military personnel in the streets. There were people being shot at, both related to and separate from the death of Michael Brown and subsequent protests. There were death threats to police officers, most notably, Darren Wilson and Chief Tom Jackson.

There was always a meeting before the meeting. When I arrived at the first meeting, the Chief had his head in his hands, hunched over a stack of papers. I believed he was resting. His shirt was unbuttoned at the top, and his cuffs were bunched up. He looked stressed, but more than that, he looked exhausted. Here was a man who one month earlier was not known across the country. He was just the Chief of Police of a small city, one of thousands of others.

Now, each day, he was fighting like hell every day he punched in. I had known him for almost a month now, and I was still cursed with the aversion to law enforcement with which I was raised. But seeing him here, with his fingers woven through the thinning hairs on his head, I knew he needed help. I bought him some more time to pull himself together.

We all took a seat at the table and got to work defining the criteria for safety at StreetFest, and drawing up any and all strategies to mitigate a crisis. This meant that we had to examine every possible thing that could go wrong at StreetFest, both so we could prevent things from getting out of hand and so that we would know how to respond if things *did* get out of hand. I was not in the meeting to identify ways to steer protest or anything like that. I was in the meeting so that I could inform the community members, protest leaders, and gang leaders on tactics that would be employed. It helped them to know that there was going to be a crackdown, so they would know that anything outside of peaceful protest would be met with strong resistance. At the same time, if the protest groups allowed it, I would share information about their plans and setup meetings with the Chief so that a mutual understanding could be achieved. This proved helpful on many occasions, despite how the media reported everything.

A common phrase at these meetings was "Code 1000." When the Chief called in a Code 1000, it meant that they needed every available cop in the area for backup. It was like a panic button, but it was also very expensive for the department, so we wanted to avoid using it at all costs.

I had received intel from a gang leader that there was going to be a drive-by shooting. When I explained this to the group, the Chief said that he, too, had received the exact same intel from an undercover informant. He also had sources tell him that there were serious threats of pipe bombs being set off.

The Chief said, "If StreetFest is going to continue, we're going to need to multiply our safety measures."

Not only would multiplying our safety measures be difficult financially and logistically, but it would also present an atmosphere of an iron fist in Ferguson. That was the exact opposite of what StreetFest was all about, and I didn't want more military or law enforcement presence anyway.

"So what do you think we should do?" the Chief asked.

"We have to cancel StreetFest," I said. The Chief agreed on the spot. He didn't want to put the community, or any more of his officers, at risk for a party with the potential for widespread calamity.

There were similar threats every day; thankfully, they had never come to fruition. Now, we had solid evidence that something major was going to happen. Watching and waiting would not be helpful. We needed to take preemptive measures. This was a very serious situation. First, the fact that both the Chief and I received the same intel signaled to me that something was bound to happen if we didn't stop it. We decided to be proactive in order to save lives.

WHO GETS HURT?

Both the Chief and I believed that cancelling StreetFest was the right thing to do. I returned to the Natta Room and had Megan, the City Clerk, send off an e-mail to the entire staff at the city:

> It is the police department's strong recommendation, in light of the escalation of this past weekend, to postpone StreetFest.

We have information that protest groups are planning to protest StreetFest. We simply do not have the manpower or resources required to keep all parties safe during such a large event. We recognize that residents will be disappointed, but safety has to be the biggest priority at this time. We would like your support on this and will be reaching out to FSBD this morning to ask for their support as well.

Thank you,

Megan Asikainen

Suddenly, that set off a tirade of internal e-mails. Council members were angry because their friends (local businessmen and women) had invested lots of money, time, and effort into this event, and we were about to tell them that it was all for nothing.

My team started drafting e-mails, flyers, and bulletins to inform every one of the decision. I gave Toni scripts for every scenario so that she would know what to say to people when she called them and they were inevitably angry. Eventually, we drafted this letter for the business community:

Dear Person,

On behalf of the City of Ferguson and the FSBD, I wish to apologize for the postponement of StreetFest this upcoming weekend.

I know many of you bring your friends and family to the occasion. I know many have secured this date and canceled other events to participate. I know you have gone to many meetings, brought and bought supplies, paid for permits, etc. and I know there is a great deal of frustration in having to cancel your plans at the last minute.

We had never anticipated that the things we have all experienced over the last few weeks would continue to disrupt community events but we have decided to postpone StreetFest this weekend in the interest of public safety. Obviously the timing for this isn't ideal and I apologize for this inconvenience but I am sure that you understand that your safety is of utmost importance and concern for us.

If there is anything I can do in the meantime please let me know and we are in the process of working on refunds and reimbursements for cost. Thanks again and I hope to secure your participation for future events.

Thanking You.

Immediately, there was backlash from the business community. One local businessman wrote to the city:

I don't know what to say, you are ALL letting the THUGS win. And NONE of you deserve your positions.

Everyone that worked so hard to put together streetfest and the residents that were looking forward to going.

I do understand keeping everyone safe. And you all know 99% of the protester are not from Ferguson.

What are you going to do with the Grand jury come back with a decision that the protesters don't like, or Darren gets acquitted.

You going to run and hide?

Chief Jackson was on the ball. He quickly wrote up an angry, authoritative reply:

What a disgusting message! Our officers and officers from many other agencies have been facing daily protests and everything from insults to gunfire and fire bombs since August. And now you want us to bring them back to face certain violence and possible injury to residents, protesters and police officers because you were looking forward to going to a PARTY???

You clearly do not understand "keeping everyone safe."

I'm waiting for a single day without this nightmare.

TJ

For every one of these angry e-mails we received, there were at least two dozen angry phone calls, voice-mails or letters. One-by-one, City Council members started turning on the Mayor, blaming him for the money that would be lost in the cancelling of the event. In reality, they were just trying to divert the fingers away from themselves, and toward the media scapegoat. Luckily, the Mayor had his head on right that day. He sent out one last mass e-mail to the council, the administrators, and me:

Council-

This is something we discussed at length already. There is no way any vendor who has paid money, bought items, and planned for a two day event will now show up for one afternoon to sell items at a modified event. It doesn't make financial sense to them.

There is a huge call out, focused on Saturday, to have disruption at the event. They will cause a full scale riot by doing what they did at farmers market, but times 10, if it is at Street-fest.

No number of police will stop what will happen. They will either shut it down after it starts or they will successfully instigate our residents into a fight.

We cannot allow this.

There was a possible Arson this morning of the Michael Brown memorial. We will be lucky to get through this tonight. The Chief and I have been working all day with clergy to calm this and be proactive. But tensions are high.

I have been completely supportive of keeping streetfest going until this weekend, and recognizing the strain on all of the pd resources. It won't be calm even without streetfest, but at least innocent people will not be in the way.

Keep in mind, if we have streetfest and there is trouble, they win. If we cancel they win. The difference is who gets hurt.

CHAPTER 18

THE CHIEF'S APOLOGY

SHORTLY AFTER THE STREETFEST incident, articles came out disclosing St. Louis County's spending on police forces since August 9. The report showed that $4.2 million dollars had been spent. The article caused an uproar among the people, who were wondering what would be different if they had spent that money on healing the community instead.

Tensions between the protestors and the police force were growing.

On the morning of September 23, news started surfacing that the Mike Brown memorial, full of flowers, cards and other gifts placed in the exact spot where Brown was killed, had been burned to the ground. Within minutes, there was a media storm covering the event, and along with that a barrage of theories about what had happened. Very few of the theories were levelheaded, but all of them held the same ground in the rapid-fire world of social media.

I was copied in an e-mail from John Shaw early on the morning. It read:

> *M & CC: FYI. M. Brown memorial was set on fire this morning. Rec. several 911 call, police arrived and was blamed for setting fire. FD put it out. Residents are very upset. A neighbor had a video camera on the memorial. Unable to get video. Had to withdraw officers from the scene. All officers' state and county have been alerted of the situation.*
>
> *PS- the media was first on the scene*

A few minutes later, I was copied on another e-mail. This one was from Marla Chichowski, a reporter for Al Jazeera America. She was writing to Tim Zoll, Ferguson Police Department's Public Information Officer (PIO). She and her crew had been covering the protests on West Florissant Avenue. She wrote:

> *We are here right now standing next to the site as well as several Residents who live here. There are several people here who have video of the actual fire. Residents say police responded to the scene but did not actually put out the fire. Did the fire dept extinguish the fire? Can you confirm? People here are saying the fire was set intentionally.*

It felt like there was no end to it. The worst part was that now, Ferguson officials would not be able to go out into predominately black areas of the city at all. Not that they ever did anyway. Councilman Dave Conway represented the area where Canfield Green was, and he never set foot over there. I remember when we were planning some outreach in the area, and he didn't even know that was his area. To make matters worse, some people blamed the police for burning the memorial, saying an accelerant had been added, like lighter fluid, or something of that nature, to make sure it was burnt to the ground.

I suggested a few things to the city at this time. I suggested that the city should replace the existing memorial for now as a temporary gesture, but also that we consider commissioning an artist from the black community to develop a sculpture or a monument of some sort in the future as a more permanent fixture for the people in the community in honor of Mike Brown. I also suggested that the city apologize for not protecting the memorial from incidents like the burning, or any other destruction of the memorial, and that they offer some sort of fund/scholarship in his honor by way of the Police Department as well.

Everyone may not believe it, but Chief Jackson and John Shaw were in support of these ideas. The rest of the City Administration and the Council didn't understand why I was asking these things, but I had a point. I believe that Brown died for no reason, and many others agreed. That is not a legal issue, but rather a moral compass issue. As such, one can feel compassion and do what's right, regardless of one's feelings towards Brown's guilt or innocence. Also there is this notion that government can't act with compassion. That is simply not true as government can be as compassionate as the representatives allow; we just have a government run by people who want to dictate and govern others rather than live in harmony together.

I was eating dinner with Chief Jackson after everyone else left. We had been talking strategy with occasional spurts of checking in with family when he steered the conversation away from everything.

"Devin," he told me, "I've done a lot of thinking lately."

He rubbed his eyes and sighed, "You've been in here since the very beginning, telling us that we need to listen to the community. You've been telling us that we need to apologize. But we haven't listened to you. I've been through a lot of training in my days, but nothing has challenged me the way being around you has. I've never seen myself as a racist at any point in my entire life. But now I see how we can all play a part in a racist system. I don't understand how people can be racist and still I have done things to hurt people in my ignorance; and that's been weighing on me for a long time now. Something inside knew you were right, but I was so caught up with work, following orders and personal drama that I wouldn't let myself admit it. I just want to let you know that I should have listened to you from the beginning."

He looked up from his plate and looked straight into my eyes.

"I feel like I've never understood the pain in the African-American community or anything they have been going through until you came in."

"I appreciate you saying that," I said.

There was silence. We both had a tear in our eye, and it was one of the most emotional moments I had on this entire journey. We are both tough guys, meaning we have both been tested for battle and don't crack under pressure so we quickly wiped our faces. I knew that his heart changed, and so did mine.

"It's hard being a black man, Tom. Some black people hate you because you're different. Most white people hate you because you're different. All my life I haven't known where to fit in and couldn't understand why everyone hates me. I couldn't understand why cops would always harass people that looked like me. I never understood why I always looked suspicious and white boys didn't. I couldn't understand why my family couldn't get a break. Why my dad couldn't stay out of jail. But that's not it, then I have my own children and I go through my own challenges as a parent. Then I wake up, and I start to see. I see what it's done to my people, and it hurts. Yeah I have a daughter but because of what is happening to black men all over this country and I have a son; I will do whatever it takes to make sure... (I got choked up thinking about my son, and stopped.)

I'm not in this for the money, Tom. So imagine how hard that is for me." (I shed another tear, and lost my voice.)

"I can't," he said. Many people don't know that Chief Jackson is a huge family man, that he loves his kids and family more than anything, so for him to admit to this was huge.

"Imagine how hard it would be for you. Imagine if it were your son or daughter," I said.

His sagging eyes started to well up with tears. He broke down crying again, and we hugged briefly, a turning point in our relationship. Prior to this, it was more like we were just two guys working together, but somehow, the experience brought us closer. We quickly got ourselves together, but we knew from that moment on things would be different.

A few days later, after a closed City Council meeting, Tom approached me once again.

"Devin, all of this started with my department and I hate what this has done to the community. I hate how I have made the African-American people feel. I've reached out to the Brown family. I know that they and the entire African-

American community may never believe me, but I'm sorry. I'm sorry for my part in this, I'm sorry that the Mayor and others don't see what we've done and I want to do what I can to make it right. I want to do the apology."

It may have been "too little, too late" for those expecting a miracle. But this apology wasn't orchestrated for some PR stunt. Anyone in the world who thinks that I, Devin James, would have advised the City of Ferguson or the Ferguson Police Department to make this apology thinking it was going to change things: think again. Ask anyone who worked with us at any of our internal planning sessions. No one was more in tune with what was going on than I. All of the people who were there protesting went home every night. The media who flew in and were broadcasting live every day went to their hotel at night. I spent the night in this; I lived and breathed it every single day. Everyone I talked to, from "community leaders" to protestors and even gas station clerks, said they wanted one thing more than anything. This had nothing to do with easing tensions with the black community or ending the riots and large protest gatherings. People were asking for humanity and in that respect, an apology was still the right thing to do first.

Before we agreed to do it, I checked the Chief to see where his heart was. I am not trying to say that I represent all black men, or that we are all on the same page, but as a black man in this situation, I still wanted to ensure that the Chief was being sincere. This was a not a decision that was made based on media. Call any of the producers, reporters or news desk that ever worked with us and they will tell you I wasn't moving to the beat of their drum. There were many times when reporters like KTVI's Betsy Bruce and KSDK's Casey Nolen all but cursed me out because I didn't prioritize their deadlines. I didn't care about the deadlines, bylines, head-lines, or any of that. Although my firm ended up advising and helping with the media relations work, our primary focus was still on the black community and improving relationships and conditions where we could. So, I told the Chief my conditions for assisting him with the apology.

My conditions were:

1. First, to try to connect with the Brown family directly. I knew that they would possibly reject it at first, but I wanted him to do his best. Since he was a friend of someone in the family, we agreed that he would reach out to them.

2. He had to be direct and intentional about what he was apologizing for. There were specific wounds to the Brown Family and the black community as a whole that I heard repeatedly. We were not doing a generic, white washed statement that didn't address the pain points, no gloss over or broad strokes. We were not doing this just by video; it was agreed that we would get him out to the heart of the black community. We needed to go door-to-door, block to block like we were on the campaign trail or an apology tour. The people needed to hear it directly from him.

When people ask why he didn't deliver this apology live or in front of a crowd my answer is simple. After reviewing all the pros and cons my team and I agreed that we didn't want the Chief to do a public address the first time he was trying to get these kinds of tough things out. Because he was being specific about certain things that we knew were extremely sensitive, we didn't want him to be thrown off by the crowd, or by the fact that he upset people before getting a chance to say his apology. I knew that the only way that he could get through the entire apology without interruption was through video.

3. There is no way that we are doing this without the end result being a sit-down with the Brown family and the community in Canfield. Since this tragedy transpired, I had not seen the city do one "official" acknowledgment to the Brown family in a way that felt compassionate. The city's posture was always defensive and I explained that Brown, regardless of how you view this, was one of the residents' children, so the entire City approach up to this point was inappropriate and insensitive.

He agreed; we would finally have an apology for the Brown family and for the black community in Ferguson.

Up to this point, the entire idea of the apology was just between the Chief and my team. Eventually, I had to pull the administration in if we were going to make this a reality. What became clear after I sent the e-mail was that no one on the City Council wanted the apology to happen. They were vehemently against any sort of public display of vulnerability. Kim Tihen, a city councilwoman, believed that the protests in Ferguson were unreasonable, and that any animosity towards one's police force showed a lack of patriotism. To her, the Ferguson police could do no wrong. If you lived in Ferguson only years earlier, you would know the name Kim Tihen as one of the officers charged in the Henry Davis incident. She and three other officers had beaten Davis, a black man, after arresting him, only to find that it was a different Henry Davis they were looking for.

The fact that we didn't have the council's support meant things would be challenging to pull together. Thankfully, the city administrators were on board, and gave the go-ahead, regardless of the resistance. This proved to be a turning point for the administration team in the city.

THE CHIEF APOLOGIZES

On the morning of September 24, we arrived at the January-Wabash Park office in Ferguson with our camera crew. We staged the room like a makeshift office, then I prepped the Chief for his speech. When people ask why the Chief wasn't in uniform, the answer is simple. The Police Department and the city would never back him and they would never "officially" do what was right for the community. People thought that the Chief's not stepping down was about his being stubborn and refusing to see things. But in actuality we talked many times about his resignation, and his position was based on the fact that he knew what was really inside his police force in terms of racism and racial bias. We both felt his assistant chief was, by far, much worse in many respects for the community, so he was trying to do all he could to reposition things before his departure. The apology on his part was an act of defiance against the empty-handed approach the council wanted to maintain. He wore a casual, collared shirt because he was speaking as a man. I felt this was key in getting as many people as possible to see that he was sincere.

He was visibly nervous. I told him, "The best thing you can do is be yourself and be truthful regarding your feelings."

For the first time, I felt like I could really trust the Chief. The anxiety was definitely still there from my history with law enforcement. I think it always will be a part of me, but at that time, I was able to see Tom as a person, and not the Chief with that uniform.

After we finished the recording, we started reaching out to some of our key people in the community about how to connect the message with larger groups. We had met them before to gain insight on what to include in the apology, so the follow-up was to make sure we got it right. The consensus in terms of feedback was that we had and that we should proceed. Since I had been doing statewide community engagement and outreach campaigns for the government for many years I knew not to go into working with the Chief to assist with the apology thinking I had all the answers just because I was a black man. I value public opinion and believe when you're using taxpayer dollars you need to include their input—but we had an important decision to make. It was a decision that would alter my presence in Ferguson and the world permanently, though at the time, it seemed trivial. We had to decide who would be credited as the source of the film, because the City of Ferguson City Council, and specifically Kim Tihen and the Mayor, were against it. Yes, there was a black man on the council but I can't tell you I had his support or that he was interested in truly working with me. I thought he could have been much more adamant about his views and supported more of the ideas my team and I presented, but he was never really a factor. The rest of the council would always side with whoever was the bully in the room at the time, which fluctuated between Kim, the Mayor and Mark Byrnes. These three were the most opinionated and argumentative, so they would always drown out the other council members.

The city administrators—specifically John, Megan and Stephanie—stood up against the council on this one. That was huge because it was the first time that city administrators tried to do something right. I had some connections at CNN, so I called up Sara Weisfeldt, Sr. a producer out of their Denver Bureau, who had been in Ferguson for weeks covering various stories. A large part of our decision to go above St. Louis media markets was because of both the media frenzy and the lack of integrity with many of the local media outlets. They should have been much more aware of the impact of their work, so I didn't want to give local outlets a chance to manipulate the story. We knew the integrity of the apology would be protected if we released it ourselves, and then the other thing we had to do was protect it from being leaked because we had City Council members and others in the fold who were playing both sides (trying to pretend to support the black Community, while in meetings doing everything they could to sabotage and disrupt anything that would support the black community. Ultimately, we decided that the Devin James Group would be the source.

I set up a couple of post-apology interviews with Ana Cabrera of CNN and Sharon Reed of KMOV at the Renaissance Hotel near the airport. When I arrived at the hotel, I rode with members of my firm, who also had their camera gear. While our camera crew and CNN's crew were staging the interview set, the Chief and I were in the lobby recapping interview points. Neither of us had an appetite, so we didn't eat, but we hung out and traded a few jokes with the hotel manager and front desk staff while waiting.

In the interviews, the Chief restated his apology to the Brown family, and he admitted that it would take action for anyone to truly believe him. The Chief's biggest accomplishment, though, came in the CNN interview, when he admitted that, "It should have been said long ago," and, "This is mine, and I'm taking ownership of it."

After we released the video, Ferguson Committeewoman Patricia Bynes tweeted to the community:

> As someone who is living & representing #Ferguson the Chief's apology helps. It is not perfect but a needed 1st step.

Katy Jamboretz of the Partnership picked up on this and re-tweeted it in order to get good publicity going for the video that they had nothing to do with.

After the interview, Sharon, the Chief, and I debriefed and discussed next steps. The game plan at this point was to end all media appearances—no more cameras. We were supposed to stay quiet until we had everything in place for the Chief to get out in the streets and address the community.

But the Chief had been re-energized. I was glad to see his enthusiasm, but I told him he would need to wait on me before he made his appearances in the community to talk with people. If he went into the community ill-prepared, he would take more criticism and spark more tension.

"I want to go out into the community now," he said. "I've stayed away from them too long. If they see me out there tonight, after my apology, they'll know that I really meant what I said."

I understood his thinking; however, I knew that the heated tension would not blow over in a matter of moments from a simple apology. It would take some time for the people to absorb it. The truth was, they would likely react with anger, and I was trying to convey to the Chief that that was okay. They were justified. They needed time to vent. Then, at some point, things would calm down, and the Chief could step in and start giving action to his words.

"Just keep away from the media and any large crowds for now," I said. "Let them react. When the time comes I will let you know what moves to make."

THE CHIEF GOES TOO FAR

That night, the Chief took matters into his own hands, and tried to go out by himself to meet with one of the protest groups. He looked drunk, but he was just having a bad reaction to some medication. He hadn't been sleeping in months, he was dealing with anxiety, and he had the wrong mix of side effects.

Either way, he ended up trying to march with the protestors, but the protestors did not embrace him at all. He had things thrown at him and looked like he was completely out of place. A scuffle erupted, and Ferguson police officers ended up making several arrests. It was a disaster, and the image of the Chief looking clueless among the crowd got plastered on all the news outlets.

Now the story was not, "Chief of Police Apologizes," it was "Chief Embarrasses Self after Apology Attempt."

This could have been avoided if the Chief had just listened to me. Although the media blew the issue out of proportion as well, the Chief definitely experienced a lapse in judgment. He wasn't trying to offend anyone, but managed to offend the nation – again.

CHAPTER 19

THE SECOND CHARACTER ASSASSINATION: TRANSITIONING OUT

BECAUSE THE CHIEF'S APPEARANCE in the community had such proximity to the release of his public apology, the media didn't bother to separate the two stories. As a result, they melded the stories together to create a new monster. Suddenly, the Chief's credibility took an even bigger hit, and his apology was not taken as seriously.

I thought the Chief's apology was sincere, but I had been privy to much more of who he was as a man than the Brown family or the public. So no one else saw that he really was sincere, and no one bothered to believe it. Journalist acted as though the apology made things *worse*. It's almost like everyone wanted chaos. The chaos was profitable. It generated ratings for shows, increased viewership for networks, reporters and journalist got awards for their contributions, many protestors were being paid, Airline prices increased, military budgets increased, as more equipment and manpower was utilized; so many were making a lot of money off of the confusion, so I wasn't surprised at the perpetuation of the negative stories.

As a result, my company, whose name was affixed to the apology video, shared the same mentions in media as Chief Jackson. We were instantly blamed for every PR blunder the City, the Police Department, the County and contractors Elasticity and Common Ground had made since the day Brown was killed. Our firm was linked in nearly every article and there were these quick captions about my "untimely" and ridiculous advice to release the video, even though the apology was one of the first and foremost things the community wanted. Think about what happened when the Chief went into the crowd after the apology, which was going to happen regardless if you didn't give people time to absorb it and react. It was a common-sense-meets-anger-and-WTF moment to hear something like this at this time, and we knew that. But I had been riding for the black community since the beginning, even when I didn't have a voice at the table. I stood up and fought from the inside, and my first presentation to the community from the time I took over communications was my delivering on what they asked for, but instead of my actions resulting in a win for our community, every news anchor with a show repeatedly bashed it all.

ASSASSINATE MY CHARACTER!

On September 25, the *St. Louis Post-Dispatch* ran a story on me. According to the article, the reporter had researched my name after finding out it was related to Chief Jackson's apology. The article "uncovered" how I had been convicted of reckless homicide a decade earlier. It went on to ask how the Partnership could have hired me, knowing my troubled past.

That article was like flipping a switch. Before I knew it, I was the new story, hot off the presses. PRNews published that I was a convicted killer, and that I was taking money from the taxpayers at a rate of $155 per hour. If I had been white, I would have received a medal of honor as a hero who "stood my ground." Instantly, people started coming at me for arbitrary things, like being fashionable, working out, taking selfies, and posting them to Twitter and Instagram throughout the day (even though everyone else was doing the same thing, but no one else was attacked for it).

None of the media outlets explained that our compensation was based on what was "allocated" to my firm by Elasticity and the Partnership, or that the fee did not directly go into my pocket. I was not a one-man show doing everything; that fee was our blended agency rate which meant I was taking a loss from the jump. I knew that I would have to make an investment if the funding wasn't modified, but this was something that I said: "If we're going to take this account, we're all in to the end regardless." We knew that no other firm in the city had the ability to do what we could, and none of them would risk their reputations and business to be a part of something bigger than they. My team and I were working around the clock in Ferguson. Do you think I could write all the talking points, do all the media coaching and training, conduct internal and stakeholder interviews myself, develop the overall community engagement plan, which looks a lot like the Mayor's "Move Ferguson Forward" announcement, attend DOJ meetings, coordinate community forums, advise the Chief of Police and the entire city every day and take all my selfies if I was alone? Not to mention, the prime contractors I worked with were being paid double what I was being paid--and they didn't do anything.

But no one asked questions about how much they were paid, so I guess it was OK for Elasticity and Common Ground to make that kind of money and more, but not me, not the black man who happens to have a felony conviction on his record. God knows we don't really want to give people a second chance in this country, because someone might actually change himself or herself for the better!

As Tennessee State Representative Barbara Cooper said about me in Memphis's Tri-State Defender, "What happened to Devin was ten years ago, if not longer. And I know because I helped him through it. What they're trying to do to him is so unfair and typical, though it really comes as no surprise. Why don't they tell the truth for a change? Yes, he was a felon; *was*. Look at what he has become since. That's the real story."

My business, my experience, and my livelihood were all being targeted. Much like Brown's robbery video, the thing I was being assassinated for had nothing to do with the situation at hand. I was a respected business owner, proud father, and student who made a firm decision to turn his life around and enter the gutsy world of entrepreneurship, and won. But no one cared. People chose to focus on the negative instead of looking at the positive results of my life.

What most people don't know is that before the article had run, I was out again making my rounds in the community. I got a call from Katy Jamboretz of the Partnership.

"Some things about your background have made it to the media," she said. "I was just wanting to call to give you a heads up."

The Post-Dispatch was a big sponsor of the Partnership's annual events. We were all familiar with them. Elasticity knew their reporters on a first-name basis, and had a huge say in the stories that they ran about the Partnership.

"Hell yeah, I've heard about it," I said. "They called, telling me they were going to run the story, and I met with them to clarify a few things."

I knew that the next steps on this project were contingent upon whether the Partnership would stick to the game plan (acknowledge that they knew about my past and use it as a social good "second chance" piece) or scapegoat me and say that they didn't know about my past and use it to initiate the termination clause of the contract.

She said, "Based on the negative publicity that will come from this, I gotta tell ya. Charlie and Denny want me to let you go. Charlie really thinks it would be best to sever ties. We're going to tell Elasticity to move on without you."

"Excuse me?" I said, "Dooley said what?"

I was so thrown off by the fact she was saying Dooley played a part in this I couldn't even focus. I regarded him in the same light as Senator Rita Days. He was like family to me, so there was a deep sense of betrayal that I couldn't overcome and since I was from the streets, loyalty means more to me than most people. Loyalty has kept me alive—yeah it comes with some dangers in certain circumstances, but it is definitely one of the highest- ranked attributes in by book.

After I paused I rebutted, "What authority does he have to fire my firm? He doesn't work for the Partnership or Elasticity. "

"I'm sorry, Devin. But we have to let you go."

"You're going to fire the only firm in Ferguson who actually gives a shit about the community?"

She just kept saying, "I'm sorry, Devin," over and over, and then hung up the phone.

I received a text from Aaron Perlut a few days later, asking me to meet him in a secret location. When I met up with him, he explained that the Partnership stakeholders had a closed meeting, and gave the order to fire my firm. He told me that both Denny Coleman and Charlie Dooley had voted to fire us. Since they were both lame ducks in office (with Coleman planning to retire and Dooley losing his election), they didn't give a damn about the ramifications on my firm or on Ferguson. If any backlash came from it, they wouldn't be around to draw any blame.

Denny Coleman went to the press, saying that my firm was let go because of my lack of transparency. He claimed that they had not been aware of my background, which was a complete lie. I had always been transparent about my background, and we even had a plan within the Partnership, if such a story about me ever arose (I'm no idiot--I knew that my past could be used against me). Also, it is idiotic to think that I could even secure this type of contract, or any of the other large contracts we've won as an agency across the country, without the hiring firm or government agency obtaining a background check on the principal owner. The Mayor, Chief of Police, and City Manager knew about my background, and talked about it publicly in media interviews. It was ridiculous to think that the Partnership did not.

The second key player, however, was the one that hurt me the most. Charlie Dooley, an African-American politician, was the County Executive of St. Louis County from 2003 to 2015. To elaborate on my comments earlier, Dooley was the family friend of my mentor, Dr. Jim Logan. My relationship with Dooley grew through Dr. Logan. Eventually I began to work in local government, and our relationship would include professional appearances where I would attend events that he would host or was associated with, and he would do the same. This went on for years. In addition to Dr. Logan, Senator Rita Days knew both Charlie and me. I met Senator Days at a Dooley fundraiser. As I mentioned, she was like family, so I was routinely over at her house for meals and even helped lay soil when her daughter was remodeling her home. Days and Dooley were close, and they both supported me. Eventually, I would support several of Dooley's campaigns, including the last one, which he lost only four days before the shooting. Dooley was well aware of my past and even commended me for turning my life around. In an interview shortly after the firing, however, Dooley denied that he even knew who I was—claiming that he had only met me a few days earlier. This was a huge personal disappointment, because the media was framing the story to make it seem like nobody knew where I had come from, even though my firm had been established and well-respected in St. Louis for several years.

Most of the local media were after me like it was a personal vendetta. At the same time, the 'who's who' of the city was in the midst of an intense political game. KMOV was one of the only media outlets that thought Dooley's admission to be strange. The night producer asked me to provide some additional photo evidence of Dooley and me together, and I provided several photos to satisfy their request. They decided to post a picture of the two of us at one of his events and one of my fundraisers. It was the same fundraiser where Dooley attended alongside Senator Days.

After seeing the picture, Dooley simply shrugged it off, and said I was a fan of his in passing who was looking for a photo opportunity. I tried to handle the situation in a professional manner, but Dooley's decision broke my heart. One thing I hate more than anything is a fake, disloyal, grown man, playing Uncle Tom. When I got the call from Katy telling me what Dooley had done, I was wrapping up in the community and heading over to the KMOV studios to speak to Sharon Reed and the night producer to pitch some new stories. But I was enraged by Dooley's decision to turn on me. I had done nothing but good for Dooley and his campaigns. Of course, Dooley won't tell you about the cash donations I made to his campaign when I first came to St. Louis. Of course, Dooley won't tell you that he, his long-time friend Dr. Jim Logan, and I attended multiple fundraisers together, and that he even made appearances with my ex. Although I trusted Dooley at one point in time, I no longer trust his word or ability to help the black community. In fact, it is sad that the black community has had to consider him a leader.

Right after I hung up with Katy, I shot over to the station and conducted my own interview on KMOV. I called him a coward on live television.

THE REAL REASON

When I was relieved of my duties, I had a lot of people back me up, saying that the Partnership didn't know what they were losing. Both the Chief and the Mayor went on record saying that I had been transparent with them from day one, and that they believed my rough past was a large reason that I was recommended to work with them and was able to help them attempt to change their perceptions, attitudes and policies. They said that I gave them access to perspectives and ideas that they would have never entertained otherwise. Chief Jackson said of me in an interview: "When a man is able to pull himself up from those types of circumstances and make a success out of himself, I think that's something to be celebrated." I just want to make it known that Chief Jackson and the City of Ferguson were never made aware of the Partnership and my firm's plan to embrace my background. We never shared any of the talking points with them at all. They all spoke from the truth they knew, which is that I disclosed it, and that through our work to enlighten them on the cultural differences and community perspective they could see my value and the value of my life experiences, good and bad.

Even the St. Louis Economic Development Partnership endorsed me to the public. They released a statement, saying, "We admire his personal growth from difficult circumstances and commend him for his high quality work in Ferguson," indicating that I was fired *despite* doing a great job.

So if I was not fired for the quality of work, and I was *admired* for my personal growth from a rough past, the question becomes, "Why was I attacked upon being fired?"

The same press release also stated, "We have asked Elasticity, our contracted communications firm, to release Devin James from his subcontractor role, due to a lack of transparency . . . it was the lack of information about his background that prompted us to make this move. Mr. James failed to inform us of his prior conviction. He also did not reveal this information to Elasticity when he was hired as a subcontractor."

The lack of transparency was never true. I was always transparent about my past and what I had overcome. I have spent the majority of my life being ashamed and embarrassed to be myself, not feeling black enough, not white enough, not cool enough, not educated enough. I've been called a failure, a screwup, told I'm worthless, called a rat, spit on by white people, and whatever else people felt that they could do to me. Anyone who knows me can tell you I boast about my being a high school and college dropout. I say things like "I had gotten my act together" because that's the best way to frame it when you're talking to the dominant culture. I had issues with my past, but I quickly discovered the fact that I cannot continue to evaluate myself through the white man's lens.

By life's challenges forcing me out of the education system, my life was actually saved. Much like the justice system, the education system is broken so that people of color are meant to fail or end up working subpar jobs where they can never get ahead, which serves as nothing more than another form of slavery.

Education either functions as an instrument which is used to facilitate integration of the younger generation into the logic of the present system and bring about conformity or it becomes the practice of freedom, the means by which men and women

*deal critically and creatively with reality and discover how to
participate in the transformation of their world.*

-Paulo Freire

The shootings in my past—both when I was shot and
when Rodney Steward lost his life—were situations that
were brought to me. I was always a responsible man; I took
care of my family, I paid my bills, I went to work, I went to
school, I excelled at both and I successfully created a company that I have run since 2004. To me, given all the challenges
I've faced and survived, considering I was born with nothing, I think I did a pretty damn good job.

DEVIN JAMES GROUP V. ELASTICITY

With all of the politics that played into my firm's firing, I
knew people were conspiring against me. I never expected
that they would blatantly disregard all the work that we had
done in the first place.

Our time in Ferguson in terms of the contract was based
on my trust in the relationships I had with Katy and Aaron.
We took the assignment on their word that the contract we
had was going to be amended to include a new scope of
work. Because of the urgency around the crisis and the impact it would have on the black community it Ferguson, I felt
compelled to put people over profit. So, my team and I had a
meeting about the risk, weighed the pros and cons of what it
could do to my firm and me personally and stepped out on
faith.

While in Ferguson, Katy, Aaron and Mark just kept telling
me to do whatever was needed. We were so busy working

229

that we never even remembered to get out any invoices, and by the time we were asked to create one, we had already exceeded the cap they had allocated to us. We kept working anyway, and wrote off tons of hours just because we believed in the work we were doing. That's a lot when you think of all the black business owners in St. Louis who have far more than I do. In an e-mail, Mark said:

> *Thanks Devin. Hope you had an enjoyable weekend. We are getting the $100K contract with Katy finalized this week, at which point I will be able to put this in for payment.*
>
> *We will need to sign a not-to-exceed contract of $50K with you, or just have you limit your team to $50K (whichever you prefer), which will include this billing. Katy has already said if we max out on that and more is needed she can go to the board and ask for more.*
>
> *I will let you know when the contract is signed with Katy etc.*

I responded with this:

> *That's cool no worries. Let me know if you got the invoice/timelog yesterday and if the previous one is already being processed so we can get some funds back we've been exhausting resources like crazy.*

He then responded,

> *I did. Both are now in our system for payment (and we are in the EDP's system for payment).*

Following the separation from the Partnership, Aaron pretended to be my friend for a bit and continued to promise me that I would be paid. He would tell me that he was waiting on the Partnership, or made up some other bs to pass the time. It was all a game. Months after we submitted our final invoice to Elasticity, they refused to pay our bill. They argued that we didn't actually do any work for them. How could they argue that we had *not* been doing any work, with all the evidence surrounding them?

BEST FOR THE CITY

When Elasticity and the Partnership fired my firm, they did nearly everything in their power to get me out of the region. Because of this I had lost all my clients in the state of Missouri, but there was still work to be done; there was still a city that needed help getting its act together. I had no intention of leaving them hanging because of the impact that that would have on the black community.

People in Ferguson's City Hall saw me as their lifeline. When the city found out that the Partnership had fired me, they realized that they were faced with another crisis of their own. They were about to lose the one firm that was doing anything right, the only one who had a real plan for media and community engagement.

It took no time at all for the city to request that my firm and I stay on board to help them. My team agreed immediately. I no longer worked with Elasticity, the Partnership, or Common Ground. That trio was the most unorganized, culturally incompetent, government taxpayer and private partnership dollar wasting machine I had ever seen. I think everyone and all of their respective firms should be held accountable for their negligence and their actions. Neither the Partnership nor Elasticity paid me for my work; instead, they challenged my integrity and decided to join in on the public humiliation and character assassination, claiming I had fraudulently billed them and the City of Ferguson for the same services. It's like it wasn't good enough that I was being labeled a violent offender based on partial reporting; I had to be labeled as a liar and someone who was untrustworthy too.

The city didn't have the budget the Partnership had to spend. But I told them, "That's okay; we're not here for money. We're not doing this for name recognition or for you; we're here to be a voice to the voiceless and help your underserved community; so you can both grow together." We never drew up a contract because we never needed one from that point forward. John Shaw and I had agreed with a gentlemen's handshake for my firm to stay in Ferguson on a pro bono basis. That doesn't mean it was without cost. This is when I *again* proved that I had been working for the community all along.

My team never even moved our things out of the Natta Room or the Police station. The very same day that we were fired, we got right back to work. I was working in the Chief's office on a strategy, assessing the police department, handling media requests, and setting up interviews with the Chief, while my team continued our work on the community engagement planning and outreach. We weren't fazed at all. We just kept doing what we had been doing all along: communication that benefits people.

THE EXIT STRATEGY

I had always held the mindset that I would be in St. Louis for the long haul, but shortly after my firm and I were fired, a lot of things started falling apart. I had been in St. Louis for nearly seven years before the Michael Brown tragedy. We were no longer bringing in any new clients, and all of our other clients in Missouri decided to let us go. When I tried renewing our lease for our office, the property manager denied the renewal application without giving us a reason. While I was away on a business trip, the landlord at my apartment loft downtown tried to evict me, even though I had never been late and never missed a payment. I had to get my attorney involved just to keep them from setting my things out on the street. This was blackballing at its finest, but that's what happens when you're black and go up against the system. Many people fear the inherent persecution involved in standing up to the system, as well as the retaliation that can impact every part of their livelihood.

I realized that our time in St. Louis was fleeting. I'm a businessman, so I knew I couldn't continue to keep bankrolling this effort, no matter how much my heart was in it, with no money coming in. So, instead of creating a plan for Ferguson to move forward with the Devin James Group, I modified the plan and developed the timeline and process deliverables so the City of Ferguson could implement the plan on its own. This plan would get them through the first quarter of 2015.

That started with building a new Ferguson. That meant acknowledging what happened and recognizing the current conditions, restructuring the power, and bringing in new people who wanted to represent the community as a whole. We knew that eventually some of the people who were in power would have to resign. They knew this too, even if they didn't like to admit it.

My team and I started drafting up resignation letters, talking points and the announcement schedule for nearly everyone. This included several council members, administrators in both city and law enforcement capacities, Chief Jackson, John Shaw and Mayor Knowles.

In a closed City Council meeting, we asked the council to have Judge Brockmeyer step down from his position and replace him with current City Council member Wesley Bell, a local attorney, professor and part time municipal judge in a nearby city. The council refused, saying they did not want to fire someone "for being white." They didn't understand the equity portion of the decision; nor did they understand how letting the Judge go would signify that the leadership cared and understood the gravity of the issue. I wasn't trying to fire the Judge for simply being white—I wanted to fire him because he had been at the heart of the broken court system that trapped African-Americans with tickets and fines. The black community needed someone who was willing to abolish discriminatory practices, and the Judge was a nuisance to that cause. But they wouldn't hear it and kept him on board. (When the DOJ investigative reports came out in March 2015, they would show that he consistently violated human rights, rigged the court system and ignored due process altogether. He would resign shortly after the reports were released.)

In addition, my firm also advised the council and administration on:

1. The establishment of a citizen review board and made the necessary contacts to national and regional organizations to fast-track the implementation. This

included traveling to various meetings in and outside of the St. Louis area to get outside stakeholder buy-in.

2. Improving recruitment efforts to increase the number of black police officers.

3. Improving relations between police officers and black youth.

4. Revising the language for how the warrant recall program, the abolishment of unnecessary administrative fees and other municipal court changes would be announced.

5. Improving and strengthening relations with the black community by:

   • Attempting to clear up misconceptions and encouraging the city and police department to be more transparent when mistakes are made. It is really important to recognize how valuable this is because the previous strategy was to deny, cover-up and defend.

   • Encouraging non-conventional meetings so that the city and police department could become "community conscious" and culturally aware. This is vital because they didn't understand that part of the division resulted from the fact that the black community was never given a "safe space" to talk. Meaning the venues were intimidating, the rhetoric was intimidating, the officials were intimidating and there was retaliation for speaking up against the system. I helped city see that they were a very big part of why the frustrations were so high.

- Initiating and developing the entire frame work for the town hall meetings the city and the DOJ took credit for hosting.

  The series we initiated included moderated conversations with residents based on:

  - Addressing Misconceptions about the City of Ferguson
  - Addressing Communication to/from Ferguson Leadership
  - Addressing Diversity and Racial Tension
  - A Roadmap for Growth: Where do we go from here?
  - Opportunities for Youth/Civic Engagement
  - Community-Oriented Policing

  Any of this look familiar? It is listed prominently on the city of Ferguson's website as the "Moving Ferguson Forward" initiative.
  http://www.fergusoncity.com/531/Moving-Ferguson-Forward

6. Encouraging the city to CONTINUALLY assess the needs of all residents, with special consideration of black residents and to establish new priorities based on what was important to each group; not the objectives of the city council and administration.

7. Initiating a genuine apartment outreach initiative that focused on low-income, elderly, or disabled residents. It's important to note that the council member who represented the Canfield area was Dave Conway, who never even set foot in that area. Whenever I was trying to plan events in the area he repeatedly de-

clined, showed up late to the planning meetings or found some other way out.

Then there was the big one: Darren Wilson himself. The Chief, the City Attorney and I worked together to try to get him to resign. I provided talking points to aide in the negotiations and added that the community (black or white) would never be at ease with him still on the force. But he and his attorney fought back. They did everything they could to keep Wilson's salary in place from the time he was put on leave, even though he had millions in the bank from his Go-FundMe page fundraising. They wanted him to receive full benefits. We kept telling them that this was selfish, and inconsiderate to his fellow police officers, who were coming under death threats, but they would not hear any of it. He was only concerned with himself. I felt that his resistance was not only selfish, but it contributed to the mentality that nearly put the entire region in danger.

We had been planning for any possible outcome of the grand jury decision. Then I started getting intel from FBI informants, local street gang leaders and undercover police about tons of violence from out-of-town gang members, an increase of military and law enforcement presence, which was followed by a conversation about possible evacuation. There were threats coming from every direction. The KKK sent a letter to City Hall announcing that they were coming into town and that they planned on doing an armed neighborhood watch.

By now, the city officials had their backs against the wall. Due to the lack of a strategic approach within government, from the state to the county level, we couldn't figure out who should handle what threats. We all knew Wilson would be cleared, and there would be rioting in the city. The more I tried to get the state and the region on the same page, the more divisive everyone became. But the government was planning for the worst, and the protest groups were asking me what was going on, as we were getting calls left and right about all the increased military presence and gear.

All the white business owners were talking about the need to hunker down and that they were ready to shoot people who came to their homes or businesses. So I took to the media myself to get the help. I needed to make sure there wasn't a civil rights war going on between the Old and New Fergusons. I needed to make sure the people all over the region knew that the whole damned state was lost and dumbfounded on what to do. Did I mention I was the only one with a plan?

All the division among the government entities created multiple silos where no information was getting in or out. Combine that with egos of elected officials and you can see why nothing was organized.

In government, community engagement planning is not valued until something bad happens, like a crisis. The problem with that is that, it's too late. The damage has already been done and there is no foundation of trust to return to. I hear a lot of folks in law enforcement say, "We're not Ferguson," or "Everyone knows that they did everything wrong." The thing is, though, you're all one incident, one arrest, one officer-involved shooting, or chokehold away from being Ferguson, New York, Baltimore, Charleston, etc.

That's why these silos are detrimental to crisis engagement, because they don't take into consideration the impact of each move they make.

Here are three plans that were never in place at the state, county or city level during the tragedy:

1. Crisis Plan – This is the tactical plan that provides the roadmap for the government to address how they should put out the fire burning in real time while minimizing real or perceived damage.

Note:
This approach should identify its impact on plans 2-3.

2. Community Engagement plan – This plan speaks to how you communicate the details of the fire that everyone in the community just saw and how you can talk them through the process of putting it out. A high emphasis should be placed on what this means to them, instead of what it means to you.

   The way things are released by the government currently do not consider the perspectives or life experiences of other cultures and is normally planned through the lens of the majority.

   Note: Even when you have to communicate negative information, there is a way to do it in a culturally sensitive and unbiased way.

3. Media relations plan – This plan is perhaps one of the most critical because the media becomes the platform that can reshape all the things the public will perceive about you: how does your organization do things? What is your culture? How do you treat people? Are

you credible? How do you disclose information? By having a solid plan that is founded on transparency and involves regular meetings with members of the community and media respectively, you will foster relationships that you can draw on that will allow your voice to be heard in difficult times.

Note: Avoid attacking rhetoric – Traditionally, when there is a story that involves a person of color, there is an assassination of the minority's character or some unconscious bias implied. This practice, along with the defensive response to officer-involved issues and deaths should be eliminated from all forms of government immediately.

On November 24, the grand jury made the decision not to indict Darren Wilson, claiming that he had feared for his own safety when he killed Michael Brown. That night, Ferguson experienced its worst night of rioting. More buildings were burned, looters decimated stores, and protesters called for the heads of law enforcement. The black community was furious; the pain was real, and it came through on a global scale. Hundreds of cities around the world joined in on the protests of the decision, all chanting the same four words.

"HANDS UP! DON'T SHOOT!"

It took five days of protests, riots, and threats on police officers' lives for Wilson to finally resign. He stepped down on Saturday, November 29. In an interview, he confidently stated, "I'm resigning of my own free will. I'm not willing to let someone else get hurt because of me." It was pitiful that he had waited so long, but more importantly, it was painful and destructive to all communities.

Some people argued that if a black officer shot a white man, he'd be forced to resign immediately. I am not here to argue that issue, but the assertion presents a very good point about implicit bias. Implicit bias shaped many of the viewpoints in the Michael Brown tragedy, and continues to illustrate several narratives in American history today. It is important to learn about implicit bias when considering current events in America, especially those that include race.

WHAT IS IMPLICIT BIAS?

In the days following Hurricane Katrina, the Associated Press published several articles detailing the strife of the flood survivors in New Orleans. In one particular case, there were two photos posted showing various citizens literally swimming their way home, dragging with them sealed bags of groceries. The first photo was of a white couple. The caption read: "Two residents wade through chest-deep water after finding bread and soda from a local grocery store after Hurricane Katrina came through the area in New Orleans, Louisiana."

The second photo was of an African American man. The caption read: "A young man walks through chest-deep flood water after looting a grocery store in New Orleans on Tuesday, Aug. 30, 2005."

This is one of many examples of implicit bias.

The Kirwan Institute for the Study of Race and Ethnicity recently published its yearly case study on implicit bias, entitled 'State of the Science: Implicit Bias Review 2015.' The review asserted that "[p]erhaps no clearer indicator of the proliferation of implicit bias into public discourse is its frequent presence in major news and media outlets...with articles appearing [in 2014] across a range of publications, including *The New York Times, The Washington Post, The Wall Street Journal, Huffington Post, Essence* magazine, *Forbes, NPR,* and *The Boston Globe,* among numerous others."[12] The article also speaks to routine police stops by citing a 2014 report by the Portland Police Bureau. The Bureau's report "analyzed data from 250,000 recorded traffic stops that occurred over 13 years in Durham, North Carolina. Findings revealed that black males were searched and stopped at double the rate of white males and ten times the rate of white females."[13] We see echoes of the Kirwan Institute's sentiments in pictures such as the ones the Associated Press published about Hurricane Katrina, and in the inherently racist policing system set up in many St. Louis County municipalities. It was this very problem of implicit bias that contributed to Darren Wilson's pulling the trigger on Mike Brown.

This is what it's like to live as a minority every single day. The majority repeatedly fails to understand that everything is different when you're an African-American, another person of color, a non-racial minority (such as a woman or gay male/female), or a person with a disability. Instead of being treated as equals, we are inherently seen as less valuable.

I guarantee you that every person of color in this country has faced an indignity, from the ridiculous to the grotesque to the sometimes fatal, at some point in their...I'm going to say last

---

[12] Staata, Cherly, Kelly Capatosto, Robin A. Wright, and Danya Contractor. "State of the Science: Implicit Bias Study 2015." *IMPLICIT BIAS.* 2015. Print.
[13] Staata, Cherly, Kelly Capatosto, Robin A. Wright, and Danya Contractor. "State of the Science: Implicit Bias Study 2015." *IMPLICIT BIAS.* 2015. Print.

couple of hours, because of their skin color. Race is there and it is a constant. You're tired of hearing about it? Imagine how fucking exhausting it is living it.

– Jon Stewart, The Daily Show with Jon Stewart.

People are quick to make assumptions, and are equally as swift to put labels upon us. Those labels are then repeated throughout the public stream of consciousness. The young black man in the Associated Press picture, who was only trying to provide for himself in an emergency, was immediately labeled as a "looter" instead of a "finder," like his white counterparts were. This parlays into the popular saying that African-Americans in the United States are guilty until proven innocent.

While implicit bias is often active, I do not believe that it is the same as racism. I believe there is a strong difference, in that racism is active while racial injustice can be passive. It happens when the deep-seated thoughts of our upbringing come out into the open. This happened to me when I was first introduced to Chief Jackson. Without even knowing him, I distrusted him, solely based on what I knew of white police officers. It wasn't fair to him, but it happened and I would later apologize to him for it. The public relations consultants Common Ground and Elasticity, the Partnership, City of Ferguson, St. Louis County and State of Missouri officials all were implicitly biased and, on top of that, made decisions with a great deal of cultural incompetence and insensitivity.

CULTURAL COMPETENCE

The main issue with many officials in Ferguson is that they lacked cultural competence. Cultural competence refers to the ability to successfully communicate with people of different cultures and backgrounds. Cultural competence is not something you're born with, inherit, or even acquire while reading this book. This competence is gained through life experiences—things that are seen, heard, felt, and acknowledged both verbally and nonverbally.

As a person who has "pulled himself up through the ranks," my life experience has provided me a unique learning environment where I had to expand my ability to receive information from others in order to survive. I had to do away with what I thought was factual, based on my limited view, and become open to alternatives in various respects. In our society, one can be deemed as culturally competent if one reads enough books or takes enough courses, if one dates someone of a different race or ethnicity and/or has a biracial or multiracial offspring. The label of cultural competency grants one the ability to work in leadership capacities, in fields such as human resources and diversity initiatives at for-profit, non-profit and government organizations. This is despite the fact that one may have never had any diverse interactions or experiences.

Simply put, the labeling of cultural competence through simulated education is scary. Without any real experience, those who achieve an academic level of cultural competency will be deemed able to effectively interact with people from different backgrounds, write strategies, and develop systems, organizations, policies, laws, and rules that impact the lives of people they have no real understanding of. Privilege still takes precedence over experience, even with formal education. This privilege bars one from obtaining real breakthroughs with people of other cultures, and further perpetuating routine appropriation and abuse. These people usually disregard issues that weren't addressed in school.

These cultural outsiders then try to fix the problems based on what they think that community needs, not knowing that they do not possess the cultural context to address the group's issues. This occurred several times in Ferguson. Even though the Partnership hired me to assist the City of Ferguson with improving relations with their black community, they still couldn't see that their own ideas were more of the problem, and were constantly starting new problems, and perpetuating old ones.

When Aaron Perlut from Elasticity suggested one black and one white man together to unify the people, he was speaking from a viewpoint of privilege. He was off base, and never once considered what the root of the problem was, or to see who the aggressor and victim were. He never took the time to see what our community really thought the issues were.

This is why cultural competence is so important. The Community Tool Box, a nationally recognized resource for community building and wellness, explains that cultural competence increases respect, creativity, participation, and trust within organizations.[14] The need for cultural competence spreads to many areas of society, including healthcare. The National Institutes of Health asserts that cultural competence is "critical to reducing health disparities and

---

[14] "Section 7. Building Culturally Competent Organizations." *Chapter 27. Cultural Competence in a Multicultural World*. The Community Tool Box, n.d. Web. 17 June 2015.

improving access to high-quality health care, health care that is respectful of and responsive to the needs of diverse patients."[15] When implemented within a specific framework, cultural competence "enables systems, agencies, and groups of professionals to function effectively to understand the needs of groups accessing health information and health care."[16] The ability to understand and effectively interact with different cultures is imperative to the health of an organization. The people I worked with in Ferguson had no true sense of cultural competence, awareness, or sensitivity to other cultures. They only worked with one goal: to perpetuate a media story. Their actions are pristine examples of the ills of cultural incompetency. Their lack of sensitivity to Michael Brown's death, coupled with their total disregard for the black community's sentiments during this tumultuous time, resulted in the public relations nightmare that captivated this country.

THE REMAINING PIECES

The City Manager and I spent my last few days together at City Hall. As I was wrapping up the last days of work, we would occasionally step away and talk about resignations and other next steps. Over the next several months, into 2015, I occasionally advised the city on different topics. I

[15] "Cultural Competency - Clear Communication - National Institutes of Health (NIH)." *U.S National Library of Medicine*. National Institutes of Health, n.d. Web. 27 June 2015.
[16] "Cultural Competency - Clear Communication - National Institutes of Health (NIH)." *U.S National Library of Medicine*. National Institutes of Health, n.d. Web. 27 June 2015.

provided as much assistance as I could as my firm and I stepped out of the picture.

John was instrumental in making sure our firm was paid retroactively for one week of services during the pro bono period, to try to offset Elasticity's refusal to pay us. It was all they could approve at that time, but it was more of a gesture of gratitude than anything else, and for that we were thankful. This was especially kind, considering all we had been through. Many people in the media tried to poke fun at the fact that we weren't paid. It seems that because I am a felon I don't deserve to be paid for any work I do, and my company doesn't warrant compensation for the services it provides. The ignorance literally blew my mind.

At John's request, Megan asked that we provide an invoice for that payment period. While rushing to pack up our belongings and head out, my team and I didn't think to adhere to the "no keywords" rule and sent our standard "detailed" invoice that included itemized task and deliverables. This meant that the invoice contained a reference to one of the resignation letters of city officials that you would later see step down. We sent in the invoice for approval and Megan sent us an e-mail, saying:

This is public record. Can we remove the resignation reference?

The Department of Justice investigation on the Ferguson Police Department was released to the public on March 4, 2015. The report showed the many injustices that I had uncovered, including a long history of institutional bias against African-Americans, in detail. When the report came out, we knew that it was time for the Chief to step down. He resigned on March 11. It was a tough decision for him personally, because he knew there were still many people in his department who contributed to the racism, and he wanted to help make things better. But he also knew, like Darren Wilson should have known, that his removal was best for the city's moving forward.

The Devin James Group eventually gave the city our long-term plan, and provided the framework for them to *Move Ferguson Forward,* which included policy change recommendations, more resignations and recommendations for replacement officials and judges. Even though the city now works with new public relations and communications firms, they still stuck to our plan.

I left Missouri in early November and flew away feeling exhausted and emotionally beaten. I needed to get away from all of the negative energy in the St. Louis area because it got to the point that all I could see was racism, bias and discrimination. Wanting a complete change of scenery, and desperately seeking more nature in my life, I moved to Portland, Oregon. I spent the next few months in the mountains, hiking, biking and on beaches up and down the coast, from the Pacific Northwest to the Bay area, just enjoying life. It was just the time I needed to recover from all of the damage this trauma had done to my self-esteem and my business. As black men, we have to work so much harder to get so much less. This fight, after all the other fights, really drained me.

But my biggest fear still loomed: that the new system was being implemented in Ferguson without a true leader in the community. It was disturbing to think that all the work we had done could crumble without the right guidance. I just wanted *someone* to be able to pick up where I had left off, and create a lasting, positive change in Ferguson.

Still, we saw a new opportunity ahead of us—an opportunity for change. The things we uncovered in Ferguson were not unique. They were common among all municipalities across the country. A person of color may be killed today in Memphis, or tomorrow in Portland, or in any place at any time. That's what the population—especially black communities and people of color all over this country—needs to realize.

This can happen to any of us. We need to keep our spare tires everywhere we go. We must remember the tragedy of Michael Brown, and the behind-the-scenes story of the Partnership, St. Louis County, Ferguson and the State of Missouri's collective response, as proof that the fight is not over. Racism is a formidable opponent, and it hasn't gone away. Some may argue that it's gotten stronger in recent years. Nevertheless, we all have significant work to do. We still face hundreds of years of institutionalized racism and bias, waiting to be unearthed. We still are searching for peace in this country, after so many years of turmoil. Our black men and women, young and old, are still being harassed, detained, beaten, choked, and gunned down in the streets, in cold blood, by law enforcement. The abuse that has been inflicted on black communities all over this country cannot continue to be ignored—and we cannot just "get over it."

What I saw and experienced inside Ferguson was reflective of America.

Find Out More

WWW.INSIDEFERGUSON.COM
#INSIDEFERGUSON

Using your mobile device or tablet, scan the QR code for up-dates on exclusive content, book signings, community events, news, case studies, and more about Author Devin S. James.